STRATEGIC AIR COMMAND

LINDSAY T. PEACOCK

STRATEGIC AIR COMMAND

LINDSAY T. PEACOCK

ARMS & ARMOUR PRESS

London   New York   Sydney

First published in Great Britain in 1988 by
Arms & Armour Press Ltd, Artillery House, Artillery
Row, London SW1P 1RT.

Distributed in the USA by Sterling Publishing Co. Inc.,
2 Park Avenue, New York, NY 10016.

Distributed in Australia by Capricorn Link (Australia) Pty.
Ltd., P.O. Box 665, Lane Cove, New South Wales 2066.

British Library Cataloguing in Publication data:
Peacock, Lindsay T.
Strategic Air Command.
1. United States, Air Force, Strategic Air Command—
History.
I. Title
358. 4'00973 UG633

ISBN 0 85368 864 8

Edited and designed at Little Oak Studios.
Typeset by Typesetters (Birmingham) Ltd.
Printed and bound in Great Britain by The Bath Press.

Front jacket illustration: The first purpose-built strategic
bomber to be delivered to SAC in more than two
decades, Rockwell's B-1B possesses outstanding
potential but it has run into a number of problems since
the first example was delivered to the 96th BW at Dyess
AFB, Texas, in June 1985. Exactly 100 B-1Bs are to be
acquired by the Command, and these will form the first
element of a long-overdue modernization programme,
which should culminate in the procurement of the even
more sophisticated Northrop Advanced Technology
Bomber (ATB) during the course of the 1990s. (USAF)

Back jacket illustrations: (Top) A Convair RB-36D
strategic reconnaissance aircraft, two of its four weapons
bays carrying a 14-camera installation. (Bottom) The
Convair B-58 Hustler was the first supersonic bomber to
enter service in the West. This particular example began
its career as part of the development batch and was
subsequently modified to serve as a TB-58A trainer.
(General Dynamics)

Title spread: External carriage of the Boeing AGM-69A
Short-Range Attack Missile by the B-52 is made possible
by a very neat pylon secured to the hardpoint which was
previously used by the AGM-28 Hound Dog missile.
Here a SRAM-armed B-52G of the 42nd BW at Loring
AFB, Maine, taxis for take-off. (Boeing)

CONTENTS

Left: A Minuteman III heads skywards just seconds after receiving the command to launch. Although ground-based Launch Control Centers have the prime responsibility for sending the Minuteman force on its way, in the event of these being either damaged or destroyed by a pre-emptive strike it is possible to initiate launch from the airborne Post Attack Command Control EC-135s, several of these aircraft embodying ALCS (Air Launch Control System) equipment. As is the case with ground-based missile crews, the simultaneous turning of widely separated keys is necessary to instigate the launch procedure. (USAF)

INTRODUCTION

Anyone who is reasonably well informed about the current status of US military air power will know that Strategic Air Command (SAC) today has responsibility for two of the three elements which comprise that nation's arsenal of strategic nuclear weapon delivery systems. At a score of air bases scattered throughout mainland USA, bomber aircraft like the Boeing B-52 Stratofortress and the General Dynamics FB-111A are maintained in a 'cocked' condition around the clock – fuelled, armed and ready to take off at little more than a moment's notice. Elsewhere, in launch control centres buried deep underground, missile crews also undertake alert duty twenty-four hours a day, while in a thousand 'holes' (launch facilities) dispersed throughout the states of Missouri, Montana, North and South Dakota and Wyoming, the Boeing Minuteman ICBMs (Intercontinental Ballistic Missiles) for which these crews are responsible await the electrical impulses that will free them and their deadly cargoes from the concrete tombs in which they are housed to fly against their designated targets.

Today, as it has been for most of the past four decades, SAC stands ready to fight. It does so reluctantly, for those assigned to the command recognize that if they are ever called upon to employ their weaponry they will have failed in their primary task of deterring aggression. Much has been written in recent years about the impact that a full-scale nuclear exchange between East and West is likely to have on the world. I do not propose to pay too much attention to the probable consequences here, since the reality of nuclear war is too horrific to contemplate, and equally difficult to visualize. There are others who are far better qualified than I to assess the outcome, although I am inclined to wonder if, in producing their statistics, these people ever pause to consider just what it all means in purely human terms.

Be that as it may, nuclear weapons are now a fact of everyday life, and from my own fairly limited observations I am convinced that SAC is as much a force for peace as it is for war. I have no doubt that there are many who will disagree with what is, essentially, a fairly simplistic view. Nonetheless, I am equally certain that those personnel who serve with SAC are far more concerned with keeping the peace than with waging war – I just wish it were possible to say the same thing about the politicians who, ultimately, exercise control over SAC's awesome potential for destruction. However, I intend to avoid the minefield of politics and will concentrate rather on SAC itself, examining its history, its equipment, and its growth into an organization which could, if it so chose, effectively bring an end to modern civilization in minutes.

Lindsay T. Peacock

Checkmate to Aggression[*]

THE EARLY YEARS

[*]Motto of the 465th
Bomb Wing

Although Strategic Air Command effectively came into being more or less overnight, its elevation to its present status has been the result of a process of evolution in which new and ever more potent weapons and weapons systems have emerged, these taking their place alongside existing systems and, in many cases, eventually replacing them. The most recent manifestations of the evolutionary process are the Rockwell B-1B bomber and the MGM-118A Peacekeeper ICBM (both of which have been a long time coming), but for much of its existence SAC has been in a continual state of flux, the far more visible changes in operational equipment being matched by less obvious changes in doctrine and tactics.

The formal establishment of SAC took place on 21 March 1946 when it became one of three major US-based combat sub-commands of the United States Army Air Force, the others being Tactical Air Command and Air Defense Command. At the same time, General George C. Kenney was appointed Commanding General, although he did not take up his new posting until 15 October, continuing to serve at the recently created United Nations in the intervening period. As a consequence, Major General St. Clair Streett, SAC's Deputy Commander, filled the breach as Acting Commanding General until Kenney arrived.

Controlled from headquarters at Bolling Field, adjacent to the Potomac River in the nation's capital, SAC's mission is best described in the words of the Commanding General Army Air Forces, General Carl Spaatz, who directed it to 'be prepared to conduct long-range offensive operations in any part of the world, either independently or in co-operation with land and naval forces; to conduct maximum-range reconnaissance over land or sea, either independently or in co-operation with land and naval forces; to provide combat units capable of intense and sustained combat

operations employing the latest and most advanced weapons; to train units and personnel for the maintenance of the Strategic Forces in all parts of the world; to perform such special missions as the Commanding General Army Air Force may direct'. This was a wide-ranging brief and one that, in truth, SAC was ill-equipped to fulfil when it came into existence. At that time, it inherited the headquarters buildings previously used by the Continental Air Forces as well as a proportion of the 'operational assets' which had been assigned to that now-defunct Command. Amongst these were one numbered Air Force (the 2nd, with headquarters at Colorado Springs), one Reconnaissance Wing (the 311th, at Buckley Field, Colorado) and a motley assortment of bomber and fighter groups, most of which were, at that time, more concerned with demobilization than with maintaining combat-ready status, for it should be borne in mind that the USAAF was still heavily engaged in postwar contraction. Indeed, of the eighteen combat groups inherited by SAC on 21 March 1946 few were fully equipped or manned and only two were destined to survive as part of the new Command until the end of the year. Demobilization was partly responsible for the demise of some, while the desire to perpetuate famous Second World War units helped to ensure the survival of others.

As for the bomber forces, SAC acquired a dozen groups which between them controlled about 40 squadrons, all nominally equipped with the Boeing B-29 Superfortress. The 93rd Bomb Group (Very Heavy) and the 467th BG (VH) were to be found at Clovis, New Mexico; Fort Worth, Texas, was home for the 448th BG (VH); Grand Island, Nebraska, hosted the 449th BG (VH); at March Field in California one could find the 40th BG (VH), while the 444th BG (VH) resided at nearby Merced; in Florida, the 462nd, 497th and 498th BGs occupied MacDill; Smoky Hill in Kansas had the 44th

Far left: This close-up view of the nose of a B-52H shows some of the appendages which sprouted as part of modernization efforts aimed at extending service life. Additional ECM equipment is contained in the fairings to the left and right of and above the radome, while the chin housings accommodate sensors for the Electro-Optical Viewing System (EVS) which was fitted to all B-52Gs and B-52Hs during the 1970s at a cost of some $248.5 million. Incorporating a forward-looking infra-red (FLIR) sensor and a television camera, EVS is a particularly valuable tool when flying at low level in the 'close curtain' nuclear attack configuration. (Author)

Left: Used in vast numbers by the US Army Air Forces during the course of the Second World War, Boeing's Flying Fortress played a key role in the air offensive against Germany and in many ways can be said to have begun the Boeing legend. At the time Strategic Air Command was created in March 1946 the B-17 did not form part of the combat inventory, but several examples of this war-weary veteran did find a niche in supporting roles. (Boeing)

and 485th BGs; and Roswell, New Mexico, was also home for two units, the 468th BG (VH) and, perhaps best known by virtue of its exploits over Hiroshima and Nagasaki in August 1945, the 509th Composite Group. Finally, Bolling Field itself had a number of combat groups assigned – the 344th Bomb Group (Light), the 394th BG (L), the 36th Fighter Group, the 86th FG and the 354th FG – but it is extremely doubtful if any were manned or equipped, Bolling apparently being one of a number of demobilization centres in use at this time. The groups

controlled six light bomber squadrons and nine fighter squadrons between them, but their tenure at Bolling was exceedingly brief, all fifteen subordinate units and four of the five parent groups being deactivated on 31 March 1946. The only survivor was the 36th FG, which remained at Bolling in an unmanned and unequipped state until September, when it was reassigned to the Caribbean Air Command.

Other elements which disappeared on 31 March 1946 were the 462nd, 468th and 497th Bomb Groups, and, in conjunction

Left: Another bomber type which was instrumental in carrying the war to the Third Reich ws the Consolidated Liberator, which is represented here by a B-24J of the 328th Bomb Squadron, 93rd Bomb Group. Few if any Liberators survived to serve with SAC in the postwar era.

with the removal of the fighter and light bomber groups, this loss, in theory, dramatically reduced the fledgeling Command's striking power, although in reality it had little genuine impact. Even so, SAC's notional order of battle was virtually halved to just nine Bomb Groups and one Composite Group barely ten days after its formation. Of these, only the 93rd and 509th still existed at the end of 1946, but SAC's overall strength remained more or less the same, most deactivations being accompanied by simultaneous activations of 'new' Bomb Groups at the same base. Thus, when the 40th and 444th BGs disappeared from the scene at Davis-Monthan on 1 October 1946, their places were taken by the 43rd BG which came into being on that date. Similarly, the simultaneous deactivation of the 449th, 448th, 485th, 467th and 498th BGs on 4 August 1946 was countered by the creation, at the same bases and on the same day, of the 28th, 92nd, 97th, 301st and 307th BGs, which possessed illustrious Second World War combat records and were thus considered worthy of retention.

In the meantime, SAC had acquired a pair of Fighter Groups, although only one of these, the 56th FG, was actually equipped by the end of 1946. Operating a mixture of P-47 Thunderbolts and P-51 Mustangs, the 56th shared the base at Selfridge, Michigan, with the 4th FG, which had still to receive operational aircraft. Similarly, of the nine Bomb Groups then in being only six were actually equipped; all used the B-29, which formed the backbone of SAC bomber power for the first two years or so of the Command's existence.

The year also saw some rationalization of the Command's infrastructure, to provide a platform for expansion in the future. SAC headquarters was relocated before the end of the year, transferring the few miles from Bolling to Andrews Field, Maryland, in mid-October, but one of the first moves, which had been implemented at the end of March 1946, was the disbandment of the 2nd Air Force, its place at Colorado Springs being taken by the 15th AF. On 7 June the 8th AF moved its headquarters from Okinawa to MacDill, this effectively being a 'paper' transaction and one that did not involve the physical transfer of man or machine. Five months later, on 1 November 1946, the 8th AF moved again, to Fort Worth, where it regained full operational status on the 19th of the month; thereafter it exercised control over a handful of units, including the 509th BG (VH), which had been redesignated from its previous status as a Composite Group on 30 July.

OPERATION 'CROSSROADS'

Fittingly, it was the 509th which gained the honour of being the first SAC unit to deliver a nuclear device, although in view of the scarcity of these weapons and the fact that the 509th was the only group with the necessary expertise it is hardly surprising that it was chosen to take part in Operation 'Crossroads'. Involving no fewer than 42,000 people – Army and Navy personnel and civilian scientists – the 'Crossroads' test project originally called for three nuclear detonations to be conducted in the vicinity of Bikini Atoll. A provisional organization known as Task Force One was in overall

Left: One wartime type which was relevant to SAC's plans during the late 1940s was the North American P-51 Mustang, this classic fighter equipping a handful of SAC-assigned Fighter Groups until it was replaced by the modern jet-powered Republic F-84 Thunderjet. (MAP)

control of the entire project, which was primarily concerned with gathering and evaluating data pertaining to nuclear effects.

Of the three proposed explosions, two were to be sub-surface, while a B-29 of the 509th CG was to open the programme with an air burst. Brigadier General Roger Ramey was in charge of the 2,200-strong Army Air Force component, Task Group 1.5, which, in addition to providing the delivery vehicle for the first test explosion – B-29 44-27354 'Dave's Dream', piloted by Major Woodrow P. Swancutt – also furnished a number of airborne photographic and data gathering platforms. The detonation duly took place on 1 July when 'Dave's Dream' dropped a 'Fat Man' device similar to that employed against Nagasaki on 9 August 1945 on a fleet of 73 surplus ships anchored off Bikini. In the ensuing explosion, five vessels in this extempore fleet were sunk and nine more ships sustained severe damage. The surviving ships were further depleted on 25 July when the first underwater explosion took place, elements of TG 1.5 again being airborne in a variety of support capacities. In the event, the amount of data generated by these two tests obviated the need for a third detonation, and most of the 'Crossroads' task force returned home, leaving the scientists to complete their observations and, metaphorically speaking, watch the dust settle.

Other notable operations accomplished during the first few months of SAC's existence acted as a kind of blueprint for the future, and those responsible for formulat-

ing policy and doctrine set about their task with vigour. One early manifestation of this was the deployment of the 28th Bomb Group from its home base at Grand Island, Nebraska, to Elmendorf during October 1946. The 28th, which remained at this Alaskan base for some six months, was the first SAC group to deploy en masse, but others soon followed and such operations became a routine aspect of SAC's first decade.

Even as the 28th BG was settling in to its new (albeit temporary) quarters, half a dozen B-29s of the 43rd BG at Davis-Monthan, Arizona, headed east at the start of a journey which terminated at Frankfurt (Rhein-Main). This mission formed perhaps the most visible part of the US response to the shooting down of a pair of USAAF C-47s over Yugoslavia and, incidentally, would be widely recognized as the first of many occasions on which SAC combat aircraft were employed in what might best be described as a diplomatic fashion. Certainly, in the face of burgeoning East–West tension, the presence of the B-29s at Rhein-Main provided a timely reminder to the Soviet Union that the USA was not about to abandon its European allies. However, the 'Selser Flight' – so called after Col. James C. Selser Jr., the officer in overall command of the six B-29s and two support C-54s from the 1st Air Transport Unit at Roswell – had another motive, since the opportunity was also taken to assess the potential of a number of overseas airfields, particularly in West Germany and the United Kingdom, as deployment bases for B-29s.

Below: SAC's modest airlift requirement was initially satisfied by a small number of Douglas C-54 Skymasters, two examples of this type accompanying the 'Selser Flight' of November 1946 when six B-29s of the 43rd Bomb Group visited a number of European air bases. (APN)

LIMITED NUCLEAR CAPABILITY

Even at this early stage it was becoming evident that the youthful Command was perceived by many as a means of projecting global air power, and it followed almost automatically that it would be tasked with delivery of the new and much-feared nuclear weapons, a mission which was formally assigned to SAC on 1 May 1946. As noted, only the 509th CG/BG had any experience of these devices at the time, and SAC's nuclear capability during the first few years of its existence was modest to say the least. The most influential factor was the extremely limited amount of fissile material available to construct such weapons, but production-standard nuclear bombs did begin to become available in the immediate postwar years, the Mk. III device – basically an improvement of the 'Fat Man' – being the first weapon to enter the stockpile in reasonable quantities. Nevertheless, the initial capability was a token one, the number of bombs on hand totalling just nine in 1946. The quantity rose by only four in 1947, but the following year a fourfold increase raised the number on charge to about 50, and it was during the closing stages of 1948 that the Mk. IV, the first standard production 'nuke' and basically an improved Mk. III, became available. Corresponding figures for the three years from

1949 to 1951 were 250, 450 and 650 weapons, graphically demonstrating the US' determination to maintain its lead in this field. It should be noted that not all of these devices would have been assigned to SAC: Navy AJ-1/2 Savage and P2V-3C Neptune ship-based attack aircraft were also capable of carrying the Mk. IV and later bombs.

Despite the fact that the quantity of nuclear weapons in the arsenal rose so little in 1947, the year was noteworthy for a significant attempt at expansion in other senses, and particularly with regard to the number of Bomb Groups, no fewer than seven being simultaneously activated at Andrews on 1 July. Unfortunately, there is a world of difference between being activated and being organized, and the only two which succeeded in making this transition were the 2nd and 98th BGs. Moving, respectively, to Davis-Monthan in Arizona and Spokane in Washington on 24 September, these groups ultimately received B-29s, but the other five groups – the 44th, 90th, 303rd, 305th and 306th – remained at Andrews, unmanned and unequipped, for the remainder of 1947; indeed, most of them were still there on 6 September 1948 when they were deactivated, the only one to escape this fate being the 306th BG, which moved to MacDill in August of that year and soon afterwards also received B-29s.

Above: Fairchild's C-82 Packet served with Strategic Air Command during the early years, a small number of aircraft being assigned to one of the specialist reconnaissance groups. Its capacious hold and ease of loading permitted it to carry bulky items of cargo without much difficulty, and it was probably mainly employed to airlift the often large cameras which still constituted the primary intelligence-gathering tool. (Fairchild Republic)

Progress was most definitely made in other directions. Several B-29 squadrons completed successful rotational training deployments at Yokota, Japan, and smaller formations of bombers visited a number of European bases, goodwill flights and routine training missions taking aircraft to most countries in the NATO alliance. A spectacular demonstration of SAC's growing muscle came on 16 May 1947 when the first 'maximum effort' mission was staged, this consisting essentially of a mass 'attack' on New York. The Command managed to put up just over 100 B-29s for this mission, and similar 'raids' were staged against major centres of population such as Chicago and Los Angeles during the course of the year. Perhaps the most memorable event of 1947, however, was the creation, on 16 September, of the United States Air Force as a separate and equal element of the US armed forces: the airborne service was now no longer a mere adjunct of the Army, dependent for funds on those who managed the Army budget.

AN INSPIRED MOVE

If 1947 may be perceived as being a rather disappointing year in SAC's history, 1948 most definitely represented an upswing in the Command's fortunes, with new units, new equipment, new missions, a new headquarters and a new commander all making their presence felt before the year was out. In the light of what followed, the appointment of Lt. Gen. Curtis E. LeMay to the command of SAC on 19 October was nothing less than an inspired move, for he, more than any other individual before or since, was to become synonymous with SAC, holding sway over a period which many now view as the Command's golden age. Renowned as a bold and innovative Second World War commander, LeMay opened his near ten-year tenure in typically aggressive fashion, almost his first move being to shift the Command's headquarters from Andrews to Offutt AFB on the outskirts of Omaha, Nebraska.

Far removed from the seat of government – and, incidentally, well away from the machinations of well-meaning but often interfering politicians and civil servants – LeMay knew what he wanted and wasted no time ensuring that he got it. Tough and uncompromising from the start, he suffered fools not at all and his subordinates very quickly became painfully aware that if they did not measure up their careers with SAC were likely to be spectacularly and mercifully brief. It is often said that we tend to get the leaders we deserve, and while SAC may not exactly have deserved LeMay, there can be no doubt that it needed him, or someone with his brand of vision, forthrightness and determination. Tyrannical in some respects, LeMay was professional in his outlook and single-minded in his approach to his job. These characteristics failed to win him many friends, but that, clearly, was never his objective in the first place. LeMay and SAC were, quite simply, made for each other.

INCREASED UNIT ESTABLISHMENT

In terms of Bomb Groups, SAC actually contracted slightly during the course of 1948, four of the seven units which were introduced in 1947 being deactivated without ever having been manned or equipped. However, two new groups did make their début. The first of these was the 22nd BG, which was reassigned from Far East Air Force (FEAF) control in May when it moved from Okinawa to Smoky Hill to operate B-29s. The second was the 11th BG, activated at Carswell on 1 December specifically to operate the massive B-36 which had recently begun to enter the SAC inventory.

These changes in the Command's assets might seem to indicate that its bomber force

was in decline in 1948, but this was very far from the case. Indeed, SAC actually experienced a 70 per cent increase, the number of B-29s on strength rising from 319 in 1947 to 486 in the space of twelve months. The year 1948 also witnessed the introduction of both the B-36 and B-50, 35 examples of each being available at the end of December. This growth was achieved principally by increasing the UE (Unit Establishment) from ten to fifteen aircraft per squadron, which resulted in the complement of a typical Bomb Group rising from 30 to 45. Implemented over a period of about two years, the increase was accompanied by a change in nomenclature, those units which operated either the B-29 or the B-50 henceforth being classified as Medium Bomb Groups, and the increased UE was confined to these elements until the advent of the B-52 in 1955.

B-36 units – subsequently designated Heavy Bomb Groups, two of which existed by the end of 1948 – initially had a much smaller UE of eighteen aircraft, but this rose to 30 in 1951. The sheer size of the B-36 was possibly one factor in bringing about the smaller UE, although it is doubtful whether it had much influence since the first two B-36 groups were both stationed at Carswell, which clearly had plenty of ramp space to accommodate them. The slow production rate and a seemingly endless series of retrospective modification projects almost certainly had some impact, while the fact that the Convair bomber was, in its early days, 'maintenance-intensive' was doubtless an important consideration. Although SAC had taken delivery of 35 B-36s by the end of 1948, the number on hand rose by only one in 1949, and by the end of 1950 pure bomber B-36s numbered only 38, with a further 20 RB-36s also on the inventory. Worse, the many problems which had to be resolved delayed fully operational status until 1951, some three years after the first examples joined SAC. Thereafter, the situation did improve markedly, so that by 31 December 1951 the number of bomber and reconnaissance-dedicated B-36s in the SAC fleet totalled 98 and 65 respectively.

The B-50 was the first item of new equipment to reach SAC, however, deliveries to the 43rd BG at Davis-Monthan getting under way on 20 February. The 43rd was one of five units which eventually utilized the type in the bomber role for extended periods between 1948 and October 1955, when the last operational B-50D was retired by the 97th BW at Biggs AFB, Texas. Two other Bomb Groups did operate some examples of the B-50 for relatively short interludes in 1950–51, while special-mission aircraft such as the RB-50E and RB-50G were retained for electronic-related reconnaissance tasks until 1956. The B-36 was also employed in a dual capacity, variants being developed to fulfil bombing and reconnaissance missions during a career which began on 26 June 1948 when the first production example was turned over to the 7th BG at Carswell – just across the runway from Convair's Fort

Below: SAC's first true heavyweight bomber was the massive Convair B-36, which began to enter service with the 7th Bomb Group at Carswell, Texas, in June 1948. Initial production examples relied on six piston engines for propulsion, four podded jet engines being added with effect from the B-36D model. The aircraft shown here, 44-92057, was originally completed as a B-36B and was one of 64 examples later updated to B-36D standard with J47 turbojets. (General Dynamics)

Worth factory, and conveniently situated during the B-36's early period of service when snags tended to crop up with depressing regularity. Despite these problems, the B-36 was the first SAC bomber to have a near-intercontinental, unrefuelled range, and it was therefore an important addition to the Command for it meant that air power could now be projected across vast distances.

FORWARD BASING AND IN-FLIGHT REFUELLING

As the B-36 joined SAC, efforts were also directed towards improving the combat radius of the B-29 and B-50 medium bombers. Ideally, the way to achieve this would have been to provide additional fuel capacity, but since the latter could only be obtained at the expense of payload (i.e. bombs) it was clearly undesirable. In consequence, SAC was forced to consider other ideas. Forward basing, in which the bombers operated from airfields closer to their targets, was perhaps the most simple method of enhancing the deterrent value of the aircraft, and, as will be seen, this was fast becoming a routine facet of SAC doctrine, although it was of course dependent on the agreement of friendly nations to make such facilities available. In the short term, there were plenty of suitable bases which SAC bombers could use, but the anxiety was that the changing political climate could well result in SAC having eventually to consolidate its forces within the territorial boundaries of the continental USA – and if that

happened the range-limited B-29s and B-50s would be able to achieve little. In-flight refuelling seemed to offer one way of overcoming this difficulty, and in June 1948 SAC duly activated its first two tanker squadrons, the 43rd Air Refueling Squadron at Davis-Monthan and the 509th ARS at Roswell. Despite the fact that experiments with aerial refuelling had begun as early as the mid-1930s, the concept was still by no means proven, and much work remained to be done to validate it. Today, of course, such activities are routine, with thousands of aerial 'hook-ups' taking place annually; then, however, SAC was by no means certain as to which method to adopt. The Command's first tankers relied on the clumsy and cumbersome British system which involved trailing hoses and grapnel hooks, and experiments were later conducted with the probe and drogue, but SAC eventually settled on the Boeing-developed 'flying boom'. First fitted to the KB-29P, this equipment became standard on both the KC-97 and KC-135, and an improved boom, designed by McDonnell Douglas, is employed by today's KC-10A Extender.

The first two tanker squadrons had to wait a few months before they began to receive the KB-29M, but sufficient aircraft were available by early December 1948 to furnish support to enable a 43rd BG B-50 to record a 41-hour, 9,870-mile, non-stop flight from Carswell to Hawaii and back, fuel being transferred on three occasions by KB-29Ms of the 43rd ARS and the 509th ARS. Essentially a demonstration, this flight was,

Above: In addition to serving as a pure bomber, Convair's 'aluminium overcast' also operated in the strategic reconnaissance role, variants like the RB-36D, RB-36F and RB-36H being procured in fairly substantial numbers. On the RB-36D depicted here, two of the four weapons bays were modified to take a 14-camera installation. (General Dynamics)

Right: The first successful Superfortress tanker, the KB-29M, used the British system of hoses and grapnels, but this soon gave way to Boeing's 'flying boom'. KB-29Ps equipped with this apparatus are represented here by an aircraft from the 97th Air Refueling Squadron. (MAP)

with the benefit of hindsight, one of the most significant events of 1948, for it confirmed that air-to-air refuelling was evolving into a valid concept and at the same time served notice that suitably configured B-29 and B-50 bombers could no longer be viewed merely as medium-range aircraft. To use the modern jargon, the KB-29M was most definitely a 'force multiplier'.

The 43rd BG had hit the headlines a few months earlier, in late July and early August, when three B-29s, departing from Davis-Monthan on 22 July, attempted to circum-navigate the world. Two of the aircraft, 'Gas Gobbler' and 'Lucky Lady', were successful, returning home on 6 August having covered 20,000 miles in 103hrs 50mins' flying time with eight stops en route; the third B-29 was less fortunate, having been forced to ditch in the Arabian Sea. SAC's third bomber type,

the B-36, had its moment of glory in December 1948, when a 7th BG machine completed a non-stop Carswell–Hawaii–Carswell flight of more than 8,000 miles in 35hrs 30mins, this being perhaps all the more remarkable in that it was accomplished without recourse to in-flight refuelling, a facility which the Convair bomber never enjoyed.

THE BERLIN AIRLIFT

Such flights impressed the public, of course, but there can be no doubt that they had a more serious purpose, although this was not always evident from the publicity which surrounded them. To those in power in the Soviet Union, each such mission clearly signalled that SAC's capability was steadily increasing, and in view of the fact that the 'Cold War' was intensifying it is probably

Above: The other new bomber type which joined Strategic Air Command in 1948 was the Boeing B-50, deliveries to the 43rd Bomb Group at Davis-Monthan commencing in February. This much improved Superfortress was produced in substantial numbers and remained operational as a bomber until 1955 and as an electronic reconnaissance platform until 1956. (Boeing)

Left: The Boeing B-50 was in many ways a throw-back to Second World War philosophy in that it carried a considerable defensive armament. Displaying the badge of SAC's 15th Air Force on the fin, the B-50D shown here was one of 222 examples built. (MAP)

fair to assume that the demonstrations caused increasing concern behind the 'Iron Curtain'.

However, the USSR was not deterred from implementing a blockade of Berlin in late June 1948. The Allied powers responded quickly with the celebrated airlift (which was, in fact, initiated by Curtis E. LeMay, who was then commanding the United States Air Forces in Europe), and although it was the transport effort which received the widest publicity, SAC's response was equally swift, if far less visible. When the blockade began, one 301st BG B-29 squadron was engaged in a rotational training deployment at Furstenfeldbruck in Germany, and the group's other two squadrons were immediately directed to move from Smoky Hill to Goose Bay in Labrador, from where they could reach Europe more quickly. In the event, they did proceed across the Atlantic, taking up residence at Furstenfeldbruck in early July, while elements of the 28th BG at Rapid City and the 307th BG at MacDill were directed to be ready to move at very short notice and the remainder of SAC went to a heightened state of alert. By late July both the 28th and 307th had transferred to bases in England, the former occupying Scampton and the latter dividing its resources between Marham and Waddington. Further bombers followed in August, and thereafter SAC maintained at least one fully fledged group in Britain on a constantly rotating basis until 'Reflex Action' began in 1958.

Even as the Berlin crisis was attracting the world's attention, SAC was holding its first Bombing Competition, an event which took place at Castle AFB, California, and which called for competing crews to perform three visual bomb releases and three radar releases from an altitude of 25,000ft. Ten groups took part in the competition, five from the 8th AF and five from the 15th, the former organization making a clean sweep by winning the first five places. The best group overall was the 43rd BG, while the best individual performance was put up by a crew from the 509th.

In many respects, 1949 appears to have been a year of consolidation, SAC's strength in terms of tactical assets changing only slightly, but one notable organizational adjustment occurred on 1 November when the 2nd Air Force was established at Barksdale, inheriting most of the personnel and operational resources previously assigned to the 311th Air Division (formerly the 311th RW), which was deactivated. The creation of the new, numbered air force at first had little impact on the general distribution of the Command's assets. The 2nd AF henceforth exercised jurisdiction over the 5th, 9th and 91st SRGs, while the 8th AF was responsible for the 2nd, 7th, 11th, 43rd and 509th BGs, plus the 27th FG; finally, the 15th AF controlled the 22nd, 28th, 92nd, 93rd, 97th, 98th, 301st, 306th and 307th BGs, together with the 1st FG. Subsequently, in early 1950, a major reorganization along geographical lines corrected the obvious imbalances, the 2nd AF henceforth controlling units in the eastern region of the USA, the 8th those in the central region and the 15th those in the western region, 15th AF headquarters having moved from Ent AFB, Colorado, to March AFB, California, during the first week of November 1949.

MORE EPIC FLIGHTS

At the operational level, the scope of temporary overseas duty increased quite significantly, most of SAC's still relatively small number of combat-ready bomb groups completing rotational tours. Activities of this nature were, by and large, accomplished without too much fuss, units coming and going from overseas bases with the minimum of publicity, but the Command again secured global news coverage with the epic solo flight of 'Lucky Lady II', which completed the first non-stop, round-the-world flight on 2 March, in the process providing graphic confirmation of SAC's 'long reach'. Beginning and ending at Carswell, the 43rd BG B-50 took 94hrs 1min and required four aerial refuellings from 43rd ARS KB-29s to complete the 23,452-mile flight, but it was an achievement which would have been impossible just a couple of years earlier and it was duly honoured by an impressive array of decorations and awards. Without doubt, the most prestigious of these was the Mackay Trophy, which was presented on an annual basis by the National Aeronautic Association for what is adjudged to be the single most outstanding flight of the year.

Less widely publicized, but perhaps rather more satisfying for those in command, was the 9,600-mile, non-stop flight made by one of the 7th BG's B-36s just a few days later. Like most of these early demonstrations of endurance, this sortie was also staged from Carswell, the B-36 being airborne for 43hrs 37mins. However, the achievement was rather overshadowed by that of 'Lucky Lady II', although this particular B-36 mission confirmed that SAC now had the potential to strike distant targets without recourse to aerial refuelling or overseas base facilities. What was sorely needed now was weapons, but at last, in 1949, the nuclear stockpile was beginning to assume worthwhile proportions, the number of devices on hand multiplying five-fold during the course of the year.

KOREA

Despite the fact that the United States now possessed an awesome strike capability, the 'Cold War' continued to become more heated, developing into full-blooded confrontation in the summer of 1950 when the conflict in Korea began. This was a fortuitous turn of events for SAC since it enabled elements of the Command to demonstrate their prowess at bombing; furthermore, it served as the catalyst for a huge expansion programme which would see the number of active bomber units double in just three years. Taken at face value, this growth might appear to indicate that the Command's capability also doubled, but this is perhaps too simplistic an assessment, because the increase was accompanied by the availability of a new medium bomber aircraft – Boeing's remarkable B-47 Stratojet, which would eventually equip no fewer than 28 Bomb Wings at the peak of its career – and by a three-fold increase in the nuclear stockpile, from 450 weapons at the end of 1950 to approximately 1,350 by the end of

Below: SAC's first pure jet was the Lockheed P-80 Shooting Star, which equipped a couple of units in 1947–48, these comprising the 4th Fighter Group at Andrews, Maryland, and the 56th Fighter Group at Selfridge, Michigan. It was the latter unit which made the first west-to-east jet fighter transatlantic crossing by the northern route in July 1948, just a few months before both groups were re-assigned to Air Defense Command. (Lockheed-California)

1953. Two new 'nukes' entered the arsenal during this period, the Mk. 7 device, which could be delivered by the F-84 Thunderjet, and the Mk. 18, carried by both the B-36 and B-47.

At the same time, the development of other nuclear weapons forged ahead at a remarkable rate. Work on at least a dozen different types was initiated during the course of the Korean War, and several of these were added to the stockpile. Notable amongst them were the first thermonuclear (fusion or 'hydrogen', as opposed to fission or 'atom') bombs, specifically the Mk. 15 which was carried by the B-47 and the massive 21-ton Mk. 17 employed by the B-36. Both of these devices were to feature in B-52 armament options at a later date.

When North Korean forces crossed the border into South Korea on 25 June 1950, the US heavy bomber resources assigned to the Far East Air Forces (FEAF) were confined to the 19th BG, which operated B-29s from North Field on Guam. Not surprisingly, this unit was soon in action, logging its first combat mission on the 28th and thereafter moving to Kadena, Okinawa, on 5 July so as to be nearer the scene of operations. Once it was clear that the North Koreans meant business and that something

Below: The slender lines of Boeing's highly successful Stratojet are evident in this view of the standard production B-47B. In an advanced stage of development when the Korean War began, the Stratojet eventually served with no fewer than 29 Bomb Wings. (Via Philip Chinnery)

U.S. NAVY #107103   USAF B-47 STRATOJET IN

more than a brief border incursion was afoot, SAC's response was no less swift, although it took slightly longer for elements of the Command to enter the fray. Within a matter of days, however, two SAC B-29 groups were on their way to the Far East, the 22nd BG leaving March AFB, California, for Kadena and the 92nd BG departing from Spokane, Washington, for Yokota in Japan.

Reaching their new bases in early July, aircraft from these groups joined B-29s of the 19th BG to form FEAF Bomber Command (Provisional), a 'temporary' organization staffed largely by seconded SAC personnel. Although the port at Wonsan was the first 'strategic' target to receive attention when 50 aircraft drawn from all three groups took part in a concentrated attack on 13 July, the B-29s were initially used mainly in a tactical capacity, operating in the immediate vicinity of the battlefield and furnishing close air support to hard-pressed United Nations forces.

Once the immediate problems had been tackled, the B-29s were employed in a more traditional strategic role, but it rapidly became evident that further heavy bombers were badly needed for the bombing offensive and SAC was duly directed by the Joint Chiefs of Staff to despatch two further groups to the combat zone. Accordingly, in early August, the B-29s of the 98th and 307th BGs, based at, respectively, Spokane and MacDill, headed west at the start of a four-year overseas sojourn.

Once in place at Yokota (98th) and Kadena (307th), these groups were quickly committed to combat, the bombing campaign reaching new levels of intensity which culminated in all the worthwhile targets in Pyongyang, Chongjin, Wonsan and Hungnam being devastated by conventional high-explosive ordnance by the end of September. A proposal to use fire-raising incendiaries indiscriminately was rejected for fear of providing the Communist propaganda machine with material which it might turn to its advantage, those in authority in Washington being anxious to avoid causing too many civilian casualties. Eventually, with little left to occupy their attention, the 22nd and 92nd BGs were released from overseas duty late in October and both units returned to the USA, leaving the 98th and 307th BGs to soldier on under FEAF operational control.

Although it was the bomber units which gained most glory in the early stages of the Korean War, the distinction of being the first SAC unit to enter combat almost certainly went to the 31st Strategic Reconnaissance Squadron. Assigned to the Travis-based 5th SRG and attached to FEAF when the conflict began, the 31st SRS was already in place at Kadena on 25 June, although it shifted quarters to Yokota on about 12 July and moved again to Johnson AB (now known as Iruma) in mid-August. During the opening phase of the war 31st SRS RB-29s were almost certainly employed to gather data likely to be of assistance in the ensuing strategic bombing offensive, for example photographic coverage of potential targets and assessments of enemy defences. Ultimately, on 16 November 1950, in one of those 'paper' moves so beloved of SAC, the 31st SRS returned home to Travis, its place at Johnson being taken by the 91st SRS from Barksdale, Louisiana. The latter unit took over 31st SRS resources and henceforth acted as an 'in-theatre' element to which personnel assigned to US-based reconnaissance forces were allocated for tours of combat duty. In this capacity, the 91st SRS stayed in Japan until December 1954.

One other SAC unit undertook combat duty in Korea in late 1950. The 27th Fighter-Escort Group (FEG) received orders to move to the war zone on 8 November, even as the 22nd and 92nd BGs were settling down to more normal peacetime activities following their return just a few days earlier. Normally resident at Bergstrom AFB, Texas, and equipped with the F-84E Thunderjet, the 27th initially flew west to San Diego, where the aircraft embarked aboard US

Above: In addition to its force of pure bombers, SAC's large fighter fleet could, with the advent of the F-84G variant of the Thunderjet, also deliver nuclear weapons, specifically the Mk.7 device which was added to the arsenal in the early 1950s. At peak strength, the F-84G equipped six Strategic Fighter Wings, each with a unit establishment of 75 aircraft distributed among three squadrons. (Republic)

Navy carriers for the long journey to the Far East. Once there, little time was wasted in establishing a rear echelon at Itazuke, Japan, and an advance echelon at Taegu, Korea. Aircraft operating from Taegu undertook their first strike mission on 6 December. Whilst attached to FEAF, 27th FEG Thunderjets were primarily used for the close air support of UN forces and for tactical reconnaissance, although the traditional escort mission was also undertaken on a number of occasions when the B-29s operated against targets in areas where they were likely to encounter determined North Korean fighter opposition. In the event, the 27th was the only SAC fighter unit to serve in Korea, spending just under seven months in combat before returning to Bergstrom in July 1951.

FURTHER REORGANIZATION
Although these were the only SAC elements which saw action, the exigencies of the war in Korea did affect the Command in other ways. As noted, the size of the force expanded greatly, and most of the new bomb groups which came into being at around this time were equipped with B-29s taken from storage in the USA. The expansion effectively began on 2 January 1951 when

Above: Republic F-84E Thunderjets of the 12th Fighter Escort Wing stand idle on the flight deck of the carrier USS *Sitkoh Bay* during the final stages of the transpacific journey to Japan. Early deployments by SAC fighter units invariably involved transfer by sea. (USAF)

four units, the 6th, 44th, 90th and 305th BGs, were activated, to be joined later in the year by the 376th BG (on 1 June), the 303rd BG (4 September) and the 308th BG (10 October), although not all of these were fully equipped by the end of 1951. At the same time, the mobilization of Reserve forces resulted in further growth, SAC being one of the commands which was augmented in this fashion. As it happened, of the several Air National Guard (ANG) bomber and fighter units which were assigned to SAC in 1951, few were destined to serve with the Command for long, but it is worth examining briefly just how this augmentation was accomplished.

In all, two bomb groups and four fighter groups were mobilized for service with SAC, the 106th BG, 108th FG and 131st FG being called up on 1 March, followed by the 111th BG, 132nd FG and 146th FG on 1 April. Equipped mainly with near-obsolete F-47 Thunderbolts and F-51 Mustangs, the four fighter groups between them controlled twelve squadrons drawn from eleven different states, but the entire batch was transferred to Tactical Air Command control in November 1951.

Bomber assets did remain with SAC for the duration of their active duty commitment, the Superfortress-equipped 106th BG (M) initially being stationed at Floyd Bennet, New York, although it moved west to March AFB at the end of March 1951. Of the 106th's three constituent squadrons, the 102nd BS and the 114th BS were drawn from New York ANG resources, a third, regular squadron (135th BS) being activated at March on 1 May. Eventually, in June 1952, a tanker squadron equipped with KB-29s, the 106th ARS, was added.

The second bomber unit gained by SAC was the 111th BG (L), which began operations with a mixture of B-26s and B-29s from Philadelphia International Airport but which moved to Fairchild on 10 April 1951. In its original form, the 111th controlled three ANG squadrons, but two of these left almost immediately to perform B-26 combat crew training tasks from Langley AFB, Virginia, under TAC auspices. Following the move to Fairchild, the 111th was eventually redesignated as a Strategic Reconnaissance Group in August 1951, a step which was accompanied by the simultaneous activation of two regular squadrons, the 129th SRS

and the 130th SRS, to bring the Group up to full strength. All three squadrons henceforth operated a mixture of B-29s and RB-29s.

At a higher level, February 1951 also witnessed a major reorganization which had a significant impact on combat units for it effectively resulted in the Wing becoming the primary combat echelon, the Group subsequently remaining in name only. Combat squadrons now reported directly to Wing headquarters for administrative and operational control, the combat groups eventually being deactivated on 16 June 1952.

TABLE 1: SAC ORDER OF BATTLE, DECEMBER 1950

Unit	Base	Components	Equipment
2nd Air Force (Barksdale AFB, La)			
2nd BG	Hunter AFB, Ga	20/49/96 BS	B-50
		2 ARS	KB-29
31st FEG	Turner AFB, Ga	307/308/309 FES	F-84B/C
55th SRG	Ramey AFB, Puerto Rico	338 SRS	RB-29/50
		55 ARS	KB-29
91st SRG	Barksdale AFB, La	322/323/324 SRS	RB-45
		91 ARS	KB-29
		38/343 SRS	RB-29 (on attachment from 55th SRG)
301st BG	Barksdale AFB, La	32/352/353 BS	B-29
		301 ARS	KB-29
306th BG	MacDill AFB, Fl	367/368/369 BS	B-29/50
		306 ARS	KB-29
307th BG	MacDill AFB, Fl (TDY with FEAF at Kadena)	370/371/372 BS	B-29
8th Air Force (Carswell AFB, Tx)			
7th BG	Carswell AFB, Tx	9/436/492 BS	B-36
11th BG	Carswell AFB, Tx	26/42/98 BS	B-36
12th FEG	Bergstrom AFB, Tx	559/560/561 FES	F-84E
27th FEG	Bergstrom AFB, Tx (TDY at Taegu, Korea)	522/523/524 FES	F-84E
28th SRG	Ellsworth AFB, SD	77/717/718 SRS	RB-36
97th BG	Biggs AFB, Tx	340/341/342 BS	B-50
		97 ARS	KB-29
509th BG	Walker AFB, NM	393/715/830 BS	B-29/50
		509 ARS	KB-29
15th Air Force (March AFB, Ca)			
5th SRG	Travis AFB, Ca	23/31/72 SRS	Receiving RB-36
9th BG	Travis AFB, Ca	1/5/99 BS	B-29
22nd BG	March AFB, Ca	2/19/33 BS	B-29
		22 ARS	KB-29
43rd BG	Davis-Monthan AFB, Az	63/64/65 BS	B-50
		43 ARS	KB-29
		307 ARS	KB-29 (attached)
92nd BG	Spokane AFB, Wa	325/326/327 BS	B-29
93rd BG	Castle AFB, Ca	328/329/330 BS	B-50
		93 ARS	KB-29
98th BG	Spokane AFB, Wa (TDY with FEAF at Yokota)	343/344/345 BS	B-29
		98 ARS	Not operational
Other unit			
91st SRS	Attached to FEAF and based at Yokota with RB-29		

At the same time, and in view of the rapidly increasing number of dual-wing bases, it was decided to introduce an intermediate link in the chain of command between combat elements and numbered Air Force headquarters. Inaugurated on 10 February, this move entailed the creation of organizations known as Air Divisions, the first five of which came into existence on that date at Barksdale (4th AD, controlling the 301st and 376th BWs), at MacDill (6th AD; 305th, 306th and 307th BWs, the last of which was attached to FEAF), at March (12th AD; 22nd and 106th BWs), at Travis (14th AD; 5th SRW and 9th BW) and at Walker (47th AD; 6th and 509th BWs).

Later in the year, eight more Air Divisions were created at other bases, including Carswell (19th AD), Davis-Monthan (36th AD), Bergstrom (42nd AD) and Fairchild (57th AD), the Air Division commander exercising direct control over the subordinate Wing commanders and the associated Air Base Group (ABG) commander, the latter functioning in a support capacity and being responsible for the management of base facilities. On formation, most Air Divisions had two combat wings assigned, although some, such as the 38th AD at Hunter and the 40th AD at Turner, still had to gain their second units.

Two further Air Divisions created in 1951 had rather wider ranging briefs. Both were situated overseas – the 5th AD at Rabat, French Morocco, and the 7th AD at South Ruislip, England – and both were initially more concerned with overseeing development and construction projects at bases earmarked for eventual use by SAC bomber, reconnaissance and fighter aircraft. The UK-based 7th AD certainly had some operational commitments at this time, however, since it was also tasked with the supervision of SAC elements engaged in rotational training. B-29s, B-36s and B-50s were all present in Great Britain at some time or other during the course of 1951, the first B-36s to reach the country arriving on 16 January when six aircraft from the 7th BW landed at Lakenheath after staging from Carswell via Limestone AFB, Maine.

By late 1951, then, SAC's fortunes were definitely improving. New weapons and new aircraft were in the process of joining the Command, additional units were being formed, the overall Command structure had been satisfactorily reorganized, combat experience had been gained in Korea and, prompted largely by that conflict, more funds were being made available for further expansion. On the other hand, US supremacy in the field of nuclear weaponry was no longer assured, for the Soviet Union now also had 'the bomb' and the means with which to deliver it. Having conducted its first test detonation in 1949, the USSR still lagged far behind the United States, but the moment of that explosion may fairly be said to be the moment at which the modern arms race began. It was a race that the United States and, by definition, Strategic Air Command were determined not to lose.

Far left, top: SAC's small fleet of transport aircraft was initially equipped with the Douglas C-54 Skymaster, but the units involved all progressed to the rather more useful Douglas C-124 Globemaster at the beginning of the 1950s. Displaying Military Air Transport Service insignia, this C-124C was typical of the aircraft which operated with SAC. (APN)

Far left, centre: Spurred on by events in Korea, the mobilization of second-line elements of the Air National Guard provided a short-lived boost to SAC's combat strength in 1951, some seventeen fighter and bomber squadrons being involved in this programme. The aircraft included some B-26 Invader light bombers, an example of which is depicted here.

Left: With 'six turning and four burning', a B-36J claws its way aloft at the start of another peacetime mission. By early 1951, after an uncertain start to its operational career, Convair's bomber was beginning to range much farther afield, and the type made its first visit to a British SAC base in January of that year. (General Dynamics)

Abundance of Strength*

TRANSITION TO JETS

*Motto of the 306th Bomb Wing

On 23 October 1951 Strategic Air Command took a giant step forward when Col. Michael McCoy, Commanding Officer of the 306th BW at MacDill AFB, Florida, collected the first Boeing B-47 Stratojet from Wichita, Texas. A B-47B later named 'The Real McCoy', this machine initiated a re-equipment programme which would continue for several years and culminate in a SAC Stratojet fleet of well over 1,500 B-47s distributed among no fewer than 28 Bomb Wings and five Reconnaissance Wings, every one of which had a nominal unit establishment of 45 aircraft divided equally among three squadrons.

Although SAC had acquired a fair amount of expertise in the operation of pure jet-powered aircraft, such activity had previously been confined to either the fighter or the reconnaissance missions, types employed including the F-80 Shooting Star, F-84 Thunderjet, F-86 Sabre and RB-45 Tornado. What had been sorely lacking was a truly effective bomber, so the advent of the Stratojet was particularly timely, especially when viewed against the climate of mistrust which then existed between East and West. The B-47, admittedly, had short-comings. It was 'short-legged' – a less than ideal characteristic when one considers that SAC's deterrent role clearly needed aircraft with intercontinental range – and it was also unforgiving in certain respects, as quite a few crews later found to their cost. Of course, in-flight refuelling largely compen-sated for the failing in range, while those pilots who flew the B-47 'by the book' seldom got into serious trouble. Such problems were, however, more than com-pensated for by the aircraft's overall perfor-mance, which, when compared with that of many contemporary fighters, was nothing if not spectacular: indeed, during the early period of the Stratojet's service, the bomber was virtually immune to interception.

The delivery of the first B-47 was accom-panied by a certain amount of 'razzmatazz',

but the orderly progression of the cere-monial programme degenerated into near farce when an over-zealous fire chief inter-vened. Unfamiliar with the characteristic trail of smoke left by the B-47, he errone-ously reached the conclusion that the in-bound Stratojet was on fire and ordered a number of appliances to pursue the aircraft down the runway. Once it had come to a halt, and with a somewhat bemused colonel looking on, he directed his fire crews to douse the six engines with a fire-suppressing agent, an act which probably did neither the engines nor his career a great deal of good.

MacDill and the 306th BW were also the first recipients of another Boeing product which made its début in 1951 – the KC-97E Stratofreighter. A multi-mission aircraft with the ability to airlift a respectable amount of cargo, the KC-97 was the first new-build tanker to reach SAC and its contribution to the Command during the 1950s should not be underestimated. The first KC-97E was delivered to the 306th ARS on 14 July, the forerunner of a fleet which eventually numbered several hundred.

SOLID FOUNDATION
Although by the end of 1951 SAC had taken its first tentative steps into the jet age, with ten B-47s delivered, piston-power still pre-dominated. The veteran B-29 was by far the most numerous bomber type, close to 250 being on hand with many more in the process of being retrieved from storage to equip those units hastily formed in an expansion programme prompted by events in the Far East. Its direct descendant, the B-50, was also in service in respectable numbers, just over 200 equipping five Bomb Wings. Three further wings had just under 100 B-36s between them, and these were at last beginning to range farther afield as Convair's bomber approached genuine combat-ready status: six aircraft from the 11th BW at Carswell, for example, paid the

Below: Entering service with the 306th Bomb Wing at MacDill AFB, Florida, in October 1951, the Boeing Stratojet very quickly established itself, gaining a position of numerical supremacy in 1953 and remaining the predominant bomber type for virtually a decade. At its peak it served with 28 Bomb Wings. (Boeing)

Left: Another jet-powered type which saw service with SAC during the early years was the classic North American F-86 Sabre, which was flown from March AFB, California, by the 1st Fighter Group's three squadrons for just over a year in 1949–50. The F-86A portrayed here displays the badges of the 94th Fighter Squadron and the 1st Fighter Group below the cockpit and possibly dates back to the brief period of SAC assignment. (MAP)

first visit to French Morocco in early December when they flew non-stop to Sidi Slimane.

Perhaps more important, though, was the fact that a solid foundation had been laid for the future, and the period from 1952 until the end of 1957 was one of near-relentless growth in terms of combat units, personnel, weaponry and overall capability. Some idea of the extent of this expansion may be gained from the fact that the number of nuclear weapons available to US forces increased more than eight-fold, rising from 650 in 1951 to no fewer than 5,450 in 1957. Inevitably, SAC bore the major responsibility for the delivery of these devices

and, as a consequence, the development of the Command was no less startling: the number of combat-ready elements rose from about a dozen wings to just over 30 during the same period. Further proof of this expansion, if it were needed, is provided by the fact that the total number of dedicated bomber aircraft on the inventory grew from about 560 to 1,655, the corresponding figures for tanker aircraft, 208 and 766, indicating even more dramatic gains.

These numbers were impressive by any standards, but there was more to it than quantity, for these increases had to be matched by qualitative improvements. There can be no doubt that the capabilities

of the B-47 and B-52 were immeasurably superior to those of the older B-29, B-36 and B-50; however, what is less easy to assess is the quality of the personnel, although here again it would appear that SAC normally got the 'pick of the crop' – perhaps surprising in view of the fact that SAC placed rather more demands on its crews than some of the other commands. Certainly, for pilot and technician alike, the job was by no means easy: poor accommodation and long working hours were not uncommon, while regular overseas deployments for periods of up to 90 days at a time were made to locations which were unlikely to find their way into many tourist guides. Nevertheless, it would appear that SAC personnel were highly motivated and that LeMay, by a combination of incentive, inducement and good old-fashioned fear, managed to get the best out of the resources at his disposal.

The war in Korea continued to dominate world attention during 1952, and SAC B-29s and RB-29s remained in the thick of the action under FEAF Bomber Command control throughout the year. At home, too, the ripples emanating from the war were also evident, and all elements of the US armed forces enjoyed a period of expansion at a time when the military purse strings were hardly drawn at all. Eight new SAC wings made their début that year. Four were pure bomber units operating a variety of equipment, the 40th BW (B-29), 95th BW (B-36), 310th BW (B-29) and 340th BW (YRB-47), and three were reconnaissance units, including the 26th SRW (YRB-47) and the 72nd SRW (RB-36); a fourth F-84G Thunderjet Fighter Wing, in the shape of the 508th SFW, was also added.

The redesignation and re-equipment of other units also exerted some influence on the overall composition of the force, elements affected in this way comprising the 6th BW, which converted from the B-29 to the B-36; the 68th SRW (M), which became the 68th BW (M); the 90th BW (M), which became the 90th SRW (M); the 106th BW, which provided a basis for the newly reactivated 320th BW; and the 111th SRW (M), which was redesignated the 111th SRW (H) in anticipation of its evolution into the 99th SRW at the beginning of 1953. SAC showed a net gain of three tanker squadrons during 1952 and ended the year with a total of nineteen, ten of which operated KB-29s

while the balance were either equipped with or in the process of receiving the KC-97. Needless to say, this gain was not achieved in a straightforward manner: of the seven squadrons which were activated (26th, 40th, 68th, 106th, 310th, 320th and 340th ARS), two very soon disappeared to be included among the four squadrons (68th, 106th, 303rd and 376th ARS) which were deactivated.

TRANSPACIFIC CROSSINGS

In-flight refuelling was at the heart of three highly significant flights that were accomplished during 1952. All three involved transpacific crossings to destinations in Japan, and, taken together, they demonstrated beyond all doubt the feasibility of the concept. The first of the flights was undertaken in early July by the 31st Fighter-Escort Wing (FEW), which despatched 58 F-84G Thunderjets to air bases at Misawa and Chitose in Northern Japan. Code-named 'Fox Peter One', it began at Turner AFB, Georgia, all the fighters proceeding non-stop to Travis AFB, California, with the aid of KB-29 tankers provided by the 2nd and 91st ARSs, which were joined by additional KB-29s from the 93rd ARS for the over-water sector from Travis to Hickam AFB, Hawaii.

The remainder of the ferry flight was accomplished in fairly easy stages, the 31st FEW fighters progressing via Midway, Wake, Eniwetok, Guam and Iwo Jima to their ultimate destinations. The journey from California to Japan took about ten days altogether, but the F-84Gs were more or less combat-ready on arrival, unlike the F-84Es of the 27th FEW which were sent to support UN forces in Korea a couple of years earlier. Eventually, in recognition of this mission, the 31st FEW received the Air Force Outstanding Unit Award, a new and prestigious form of commendation.

In contrast, Major Louis Carrington and his crew had to make do with the Mackay Trophy, which they received for the first non-stop flight from Elmendorf to Yokota. Accomplished in an RB-45C of the 91st SRW on 29 July, two refuelling 'hook-ups' with KB-29s made this solo trip possible. Mass movement was again the order of the day for 'Fox Peter Two', which involved the transfer of 75 27th FEW F-84Gs from Bergstrom to Misawa in early October so as to

relieve the 31st FEW which had completed its 90-day rotational training tour. Employing the same basic route as had the 31st in July, the 27th staged via Travis, Hickam and Midway, thereafter utilizing in-flight refuelling by a pre-positioned tanker task force to permit the Midway–Misawa sector to be accomplished non-stop, a process which should have taken about two days off the transit time. Unfortunately, bad weather intervened at Hickam and Midway.

SAC's 1952 Bombing Competition included a team from the Royal Air Force for the second year in succession. Flying B-29 Washingtons and Avro Lincolns, it failed to bring home any silverware, but the event was notable in that it ended in a tie, with the 93rd and 97th BWs sharing top honours. In consequence, each of these B-50D wings held the Fairchild Trophy for six months. Not to be outdone, the growing reconnaissance community also entered into competition for the first time in 1952, this new meet, which took place in late October, being more correctly known as the SAC Reconnaissance, Photo and Navigation

Competition. Four of SAC's nine reconnaissance-dedicated wings competed, RB-45s and RB-50s operating from Lockbourne and the RB-36s from Rapid City. Each of the competing units was allowed to enter three crews, and the 28th SRW eventually emerged victorious, possibly benefiting from the fact that their RB-36s were flying over familiar ground since the unit was normally resident at Rapid City. For achieving the highest combined score in photographic reconnaissance and navigation, the 28th won the P. T. Cullen Award, named in memory of Brig. Gen. Cullen who, before his death in March 1951, had been acknowledged as an expert in the field of photographic reconnaissance.

STRATOJETS PROLIFERATE

The year 1953 witnessed the end of the Korean War, a cease-fire coming into effect on 27 July. In the course of this long conflict, B-29s operating from bases in Japan and on Okinawa flew more than 21,000 combat sorties, during which no less than 167,100 tons of bombs were dropped on targets ranging across the length and breadth of North Korea. As SAC's first exposure to the realities of war, the campaign offered a valuable opportunity to test the mettle of the Command's combat-rated aircrews. The end of hostilities had little impact on its organization, however, most of the bomber units and personnel resources attached to FEAF Bomber Command remaining in the Far East until well

into 1954. In contrast, big changes were afoot at home: the size of the Stratojet force began to increase rapidly as production of Boeing's medium bomber got into its stride, and the number on hand at the end of the year had passed 400; more importantly, the B-47 was now considered to be fully operational, the 306th Bomb Wing's summer rotational training deployment to Fairford, England, having marked the arrival of SAC's newest bomber as part of the deterrent force.

Movement from MacDill to Fairford was accomplished in squadron-sized elements, departure from the Florida base taking place over the period 3–5 June. Each cell of fifteen B-47Bs stopped overnight at Limestone AFB, Maine (now known as Loring AFB), before proceeding across the Atlantic Ocean to Britain, where they were to remain for some 90 days. Inevitably, records were broken repeatedly, the 45th B-47 to arrive signalling the end of the deployment phase by crossing the ocean in only 5hrs 22mins, at an average speed of about 575mph. KC-97 tanker/transport aircraft of the associated 306th ARS also came to Britain in support of the B-47s, staging via Harmon in Newfoundland en route to their deployment base at Mildenhall.

Brize Norton was the next British airfield to feel the weight of the B-47, MacDill's second Stratojet wing, the 305th BW, arriving for a 90-day stay when it relieved the 306th in September. The 305th in turn gave way to the 22nd BW which was transferred

Above: Close links were very quickly forged between SAC and RAF Bomber Command. For the 1952 SAC Bombing Competition the RAF despatched a number of Lincoln and B-29 Washington aircraft to the USA, an example of the latter type, from No. 115 Squadron at Marham, Norfolk, being seen here. (MAP)

Right: Pictured against the impressive backdrop of the Grand Coulee Dam, 49-2701 was one of seventeen new-build RB-36Ds, a further seven being made available to SAC through the conversion of existing B-36Bs. The production of some 120 RB-36Es, RB-36Fs and RB-36Hs permitted SAC to assign reconnaissance-dedicated derivatives of this bomber to four Strategic Reconnaissance Wings between 1950 and 1955. (General Dynamics)

from March AFB to Upper Heyford in December, and thereafter at least one B-47 wing was to be kept in temporary residence at British air bases until early in 1958, when SAC's wing rotation policy was abandoned in favour of the more effective 'Reflex Action' system of bomber deployment. Wing-sized visits by B-47 units were by no means confined to Britain, however: bases in French Morocco, most notably those at Sidi Slimane and Ben Guerir, hosted the Stratojet on numerous occasions in the mid-1950s, as too did Andersen AFB, Guam, and Elmendorf AFB in Alaska.

OPERATION 'LONGSTRIDE'

The year 1953 was indeed a memorable one for deployments, and several types of aircraft ranged far and wide as SAC sought to confirm its arrival as an instrument of deterrence and a force for peace. Perhaps the single most dramatic demonstration of the Command's increasing power came with Operation 'Longstride', when, during August, two separate flights of F-84G Thunderjets completed the first mass non-stop Atlantic crossing by fighter aircraft. In order more clearly to understand the significance of this event, it is necessary to go back to the beginning of the year. On 20 January, SAC's four Fighter-Escort Wings were redesignated Strategic Fighter Wings (SFWs) in anticipation of acquiring a nuclear strike capability. This important additional responsibility brought with it a need for rapid deployment, and a key feature of the 'Longstride' exercise was to show that this was now a feasible proposition. Accomplished by elements of the 31st and 508th Strategic Fighter Wings from Turner AFB, Georgia, with the aid of inflight refuelling, 'Longstride' was managed by the co-located 40th Air Division and duly got under way on 20 August when Col. David Schilling, the 31st SFW commander, took off from Turner in company with eight other F-84Gs and headed east. Shedding a spare aircraft at Savannah, the formation continued out across the Atlantic, keeping an in-flight refuelling rendezvous with KC-97 tankers operating from Kindley in Bermuda and Lajes in the Azores on three occasions. Nouasseur in French Morocco, the ultimate destination, was reached safely by all eight aircraft and the flying time amounted to 10hrs 20mins.

The second phase of the operation was, if anything, more ambitious, involving a total of twenty aircraft led by the 40th AD commanding officer, Col. Thayer Olds, and Col. Cy Wilson of the 508th SFW. Once again, three refuelling 'hook-ups' were accomplished en route, KB-29s of the 100th ARS dispensing fuel near Boston, KC-97s of the 26th ARS providing fuel near Labrador and KC-97s of the 306th ARS handling the last contact near Iceland. The flight time was approximately 11hrs 20mins, and seventeen of the twenty Thunderjets completed the trip non-stop, three others having to divert to Keflavik although they did eventually meet up with their colleagues at their UK destination, RAF Lakenheath. All 28 F-84Gs involved in 'Longstride' returned safely to Turner in early September, the 40th AD later being awarded the Mackay Trophy in recognition of its achievement – which cleared the way for regular, non-stop, transatlantic crossings by fighter aircraft.

Such pioneering flights were by no means confined to the F-84 and B-47 communities, although in view of the publicity they received they undoubtedly provided the most visible evidence of SAC's increasingly long reach. The B-36 also flew some impressive missions in 1953, perhaps the most significant being a mass visit by aircraft of the Fairchild-based 92nd BW to USAF facilities in Japan, Okinawa and Guam during August and September. Little more than a year later, in October 1954, the 92nd again broke new ground when it made the first wing-sized B-36 deployment to an overseas base, spending 90 days at Andersen AFB, Guam.

The number of active combat wings increased only slightly during 1953 – indeed, apart from a deactivation and activation exercise which resulted in the 111th SRW evolving into the RB-36-equipped 99th

Above: Seen at one of the British SAC bases on a typically damp day, a 'dayglo' be-decked KC-97G undertakes 'strip alert' duty in the early 1960s. By that time, the portly 'Strat' had been largely replaced by the jet-powered KC-135A Stratotanker, although it was not until December 1965 that the last examples were retired by SAC. (APN)

Far left: Roughly one-quarter of the 90 Stratojets which were assigned to March AFB, California, are visible in this 1956 view of the hard standing at that base. Aircraft in the foreground display the 320th BW's diagonal stripe fin marking, while those in the distance are from the 22nd BW. Scenes like this were typical of several SAC installations in the USA. (Joe Bruch via Paul Bennett)

SRW, only four new wings appeared, and two of these, the 407th and 506th SFWs, were fighter units destined to operate Republic's nuclear-capable F-84G Thunderjet. Two more bomber units also made their début, one, the 42nd BW, being created to utilize Convair's B-36 and the other, the 321st BW, acquiring the B-47. As for the increasingly important tanker fleet, the year witnessed a net gain of nine squadrons, most of which were equipped with the Boeing KC-97. By the end of 1953 this aircraft had become the most numerous type on SAC's steadily rising inventory, with some 359 examples on strength.

If 1953 were a year of only modest growth, the same could most certainly not be said of 1954, which witnessed a considerable infusion of new equipment and a spectacular increase in the number of

tactical resources. About 800 more aircraft entered service, and the total rose above 2,500 as more new B-47s and RB-47s flooded in from the three production centres. The increasing availability of jet-powered equipment also heralded the end of the line for the B-29 as a pure bomber aircraft, the last few units disposing of their remaining equipment as the year progressed, leaving only the KB-29 to recall the days when the trusty 'Superfort' fulfilled SAC's primary deterrent role. Piston-engined aircraft did, nonetheless, continue to form an important part of SAC's resources, the B-36 and B-50 remaining in service with a number of units, while the tanker fleet was wholly equipped with such types – most notably the KC-97, of which no fewer than 592 examples were on hand at the end of the year. Fighter resources also rose considerably, the swept-wing Thunderstreak making its début with the 506th SFW at Dow AFB, Maine, during January. By the end of 1954 many of the 411 F-84s on charge were of this sub-type.

Despite the significant influx of new equipment, the number of combat wings within the Command increased by only two. One, the 19th BW at Pinecastle AFB, Florida, was transferred from FEAF Bomber Command in June, shortly before that organization stood down, and the responsibility for managing bomber resources in that part of the world was henceforth entrusted to SAC's 3rd Air Division, which was activated at Andersen AFB, Guam, in mid-June. Bomber assets under 3rd AD control initially comprised the B-29s of the 98th and 307th BWs, but both units returned to the USA in the latter half of the year, disposing of their veteran B-29s at Davis-Monthan before proceeding to Lincoln AFB, Nebraska, where they were soon equipped with the B-47. SAC's second new wing was the 96th BW, which had in fact been activated at Altus AFB, Oklahoma, in November the previous year. The 96th remained dormant for some months, more or less unmanned, until it began acquiring KC-97s in the spring of 1954, and it had to wait another year before re-equipping with the B-47.

With such a massive infusion of new equipment, it was hardly surprising that the Stratojet tended to hog the limelight during 1954, three particularly memorable flights

providing graphic confirmation that, with the aid of in-flight refuelling, the B-47 could fairly be described as an intercontinental bomber. The first of these flights occurred in the latter half of June, when a trio of 22nd BW aircraft flew non-stop from March AFB to Yokota, Japan, completing the 6,700-mile journey in about 15 hours with the aid of two aerial 'drinks' furnished by KC-97s. At that time the longest point-to-point, non-stop B-47 flight, it was also the Stratojet's first visit to the Far East, but the event paled into near insignificance when compared with one aspect of Operation 'Leap Frog'.

Involving both of the 38th AD's B-47 wings (the 2nd and the 308th), 'Leap Frog' was mainly intended to evaluate a new method of intercontinental bombing operations and required B-47s flying from Hunter AFB, Georgia, to undertake simulated attacks against 'targets' in Europe, missions of this type terminating with 'post-strike' recovery at one of the North African SAC bases. In-flight refuelling was, naturally, of paramount importance if this concept were to prove successful, but two aircraft of the 308th BW took matters a stage further when, in early August, they left Hunter, flew non-stop to Morocco, attacked a 'target', and then returned directly to the home base in Georgia. Operating independently, each B-47 required four refuellings while airborne, one spending just over 24 hours aloft and the other 25 hours 23 minutes to complete the 10,000-mile trip. Not surprisingly, this meritorious flight earned the 308th BW the Mackay Trophy for 1954, but an even more remarkable mission made in mid-November seems to have gone unrewarded, perhaps because it was unplanned. Departing from Sidi Slimane in Morocco at the start of what should have been a routine flight, Col. David Burchinal of the 43rd BW had the misfortune to find his destination airfield, Fairford, closed because of bad weather, and he elected to return to Sidi Slimane, only to find that base out of operation as well. Eventually, the weather relented sufficiently to permit a landing at Fairford, Burchinal and his crew in the meantime having flown continuously for 47hrs 35mins, logged no less than 21,163 miles and completed some nine in-flight refuellings in what was an impressive display of endurance on the part of both man and machine.

THE STRATOFORTRESS ARRIVES

In terms of equipment, the single most important event of 1955 was without doubt the delivery of the first example of Boeing's massive, eight-engined B-52 Stratofortress on 29 June, the aircraft concerned being ferried from Seattle to Castle AFB, California by the commanding officer of the 93rd BW, Brig. Gen. William E. Eubank Jr. The forerunner of a fleet which eventually numbered well over 600, this B-52B had been joined by a further seventeen aircraft by the end of 1955, while another nail was hammered into the coffin of piston-power in October when the last B-50D was retired by the 97th BW at Biggs AFB, Texas. Although no longer employed as pure bombers, some RB-50s – and, indeed, even a few ERB-29s – remained active until about May 1956, these being engaged on highly specialized, top secret, electronic reconnaissance missions, which were in time largely consolidated under the control of the 55th SRW at Forbes AFB, Kansas.

Piston-engined bombers did not disappear completely from the scene at this time, since variants of the B-36 had a few more years of service left. One noteworthy happening late in the year was the redesignation of SAC's four heavy Strategic Reconnaissance Wings as heavy Bomb Wings on 1 October, a change which merely formalized a decision taken just over a year earlier, in June 1955, to assign bombing duties to those units equipped with the RB-36. The squadrons did retain a reconnaissance capability, but this was viewed very much as a secondary mission and one which diminished in importance as the decade progressed.

Against this background, the pure bomber B-47 fleet continued to grow, passing 1,000 aircraft during the course of a year which also saw the activation of four new wings (the 341st, 379th, 380th and 384th BWs), as well as another reconnaissance-dedicated unit (the 70th SRW) equipped with the RB-47E. The year 1955 also showed a net gain of six tanker squadrons and a commensurate increase in the number of KC-97s to just under 700, about 80 KB-29s also remaining active throughout the year. Even more importantly, though, 1955 was notable for a shift in policy with regard to the deployment of tanker aircraft, prompted largely by a desire to increase tanker resources in the strategically important extreme north-eastern USA, which was, of course, a key staging area for units engaged in rotational training to bases in Europe and North Africa and a vital one in the event of SAC's bombers' being committed to war. Bases like Goose Bay, Harmon and Thule supported KC-97 squadrons on a continuously rotating pattern, but these units were hard pressed to meet the demand for tanker support and SAC therefore set about establishing Air Refueling Wings (ARWs), the first two of which came into being on 1 April. Both were situated in the north-east, the 4050th ARW at Westover AFB, Massachusetts, and the 4060th ARW at Dow AFB, Maine, and each of them exercised control over two KC-97 squadrons.

Less obvious, but no less important, was a Command-wide reorganization accomplished in mid-summer, mainly as a result of the increasing number of SAC assets present in the north-eastern states. Perhaps the most visible manifestation of this was the movement of the 8th AF's headquarters from Carswell AFB, Texas, to Westover on 13 June, which necessitated a drastic realignment of the three numbered air forces which constituted intermediate links in SAC's chain of command. Although still organized generally along geographical lines, the areas of responsibility changed considerably, the 2nd AF at Barksdale henceforth looking after the south-eastern USA, including Texas, while the 8th AF at Westover was tasked with managing the north-east and central portion. Finally, the 15th AF at March exercised command jurisdiction over those bases and units located in the west and south-west.

The year 1956 may fairly be said to have marked the beginning of the end for the Convair B-36, the number of operational aircraft declining during the course of the year as more and more B-52s entered service. SAC's first B-52 wing – the 93rd at Castle, which had previously operated the B-47 – had received its full initial complement of 30 aircraft (later increased to 45) by March 1956 and thereafter functioned mainly in the training role, but the next few units to convert were all formerly equipped with B-36s; Loring's 42nd BW led the way when it began to take delivery of the Stratofortress in June.

In common with all the early B-52 wings, the 42nd was initially organized as a three-squadron unit with a complement of 45 aircraft, and, production of the 'Buff' being undertaken by Boeing factories at Seattle and Wichita, sufficient aircraft were available to permit the re-equipping of the 99th BW to begin in December, this unit having been non-operational since moving from Fairchild to Westover in early September. Never slow to display the capabilities of its new equipment, SAC staged an impressive demonstration in late November, when eight Stratofortresses drawn from the 42nd and 93rd BWs carried out Operation 'Quck Kick', which was essentially a non-stop flight around the boundaries of the North American land mass.

THE SUEZ CRISIS

More significant in terms of demonstrating SAC's awesome retaliatory capability was a pair of co-ordinated exercises completed at the beginning of December against a background of increasing world tension brought about by the Suez crisis. Some of the elements involved in 'Power House' and 'Road Block' actually formed part of SAC's response to Suez. The Command wasted little time boosting tanker resources in key areas, KC-97 squadrons on rotational deployments being used to establish task forces at major bases in the northern USA, Greenland, Labrador and Newfoundland. Elsewhere, bomber forces deployed to overseas bases as part of the rotational training programme also assumed a heightened alert status, units involved comprising the 306th BW at Ben Guerir, the 310th BW at Greenham Common and the 320th BW at Andersen, all three equipped with the B-47. The RB-47 reconnaissance bombers of the 70th SRW were present at Sidi Slimane when the crisis broke, having arrived there on 26 October in a move which may have been fortuitous but was probably not unconnected with what followed. 'Power House' and 'Road Block' involved more than 1,000 aircraft – predominantly B-47s and KC-97s – and took the form of simulated combat missions, the skies above North America and the Arctic acting as the 'playground' for the largest exercise thus far undertaken by SAC.

The eighth SAC bomber meet was held in August and took the form of a combined

bombing, navigation and reconnaissance event. Although dominated by the numerically superior B-47 fleet, B-52s from the 42nd and 93rd BWs did mark the début of the Stratofortress in competitive flying, but the aircraft failed to win any prizes. The 1956 meeting represented the B-36's swansong in that the prestigious Fairchild Trophy was won by the 11th BW, while the 91st SRW's RB-47Es claimed the P. T. Cullen Award. Fighter forces were also engaged in

TABLE 2: SAC ORDER OF BATTLE, DECEMBER 1956

Division	Base	Unit	Components	Equipment
2nd Air Force (Barksdale AFB, La)				
4th AD	Barksdale AFB, La	301st BW	32/352/353 BS	B-47
			301 ARS	KC-97
		376th BW	512/513/514 BS	B-47
			376 ARS	KC-97
6th AD	MacDill AFB, Fl	305th BW	364/365/366 BS	B-47
			305 ARS	KC-97
		306th BW	367/368/369 BS	B-47
			306 ARS	KC-97
19th AD	Carswell AFB, Tx	7th BW	9/436/492 BS	B-36
		11th BW	26/42/98 BS	B-36
38th AD	Hunter AFB, Ga	2nd BW	20/49/96 BS	B-47
			2 ARS	KC-97
		308th BW	373/374/375 BS	B-47
			303 ARS	KC-97 (attached but at Kindley, Bermuda)
			308 ARS	KC-97
40th AD	Turner AFB, Ga	31st SFW	307/308/309 SFS	F-84F
			508 ARS	KB-29P
		4080th SRW	4025/4028 SRS	RB-57D
			4029 SRS	Not equipped
42nd AD	Bergstrom AFB, Tx	12th SFW	559/560/561 SFS	F-84F
			506 ARS	KB-29P (attached)
		27th SFW	522/523/524 SFS	F-84F
			27 ARS	KB-29P
806th AD	Chennault AFB, La	44th BW	66/67/68 BS	B-47
			44 ARS	KC-97
		68th BW	51/52/656 BS	B-47
			68 ARS	KC-97
823rd AD	Homestead AFB, Fl	19th BW	28/30/93 BS	B-47
			19 ARS	KC-97
		379th BW	524/525/526 BS	B-47
825th AD	Little Rock AFB, Ar	70th SRW	6/26/61 SRS	RB-47E
			70 ARS	KC-97
		384th BW	544/545/546 BS	B-47
–	Ramey AFB, Puerto Rico	72nd BW	60/73/301 BS	RB-36
–	McCoy AFB, Fl	321st BW	445/446/447 BS	B-47
–	Tinker AFB, Ok	506th SFW	457/458/462 SFS	F-84F
8th Air Force (Westover AFB, Ma)				
21st AD	Forbes AFB, Ks	55th SRW	38/338/343 SRS	RB-47H
			55 ARS	KC-97
		90th SRW	319/320/321 SRS	RB-47E
			90 ARS	KC-97

Continued on p. 39

competition for the first time, Operation 'Left Hook' being staged from Offutt AFB, Nebraska, between late October and mid-November. Five wings took part, the 508th SFW having been deactivated in May, and each despatched 36 F-84Fs to Offutt in succession. The Tinker-based 506th SFW emerged victorious and won the Auton Trophy, but this competition was staged only once, falling victim to the phasing out of fighter aircraft from SAC in 1957.

In terms of Command organization, 1956 brought little change. Two new wings appeared, however, and both were significant, but for very different reasons. One, the 100th BW based at Pease, New Hampshire, more or less marked the end of the B-47 transition programme: it was the 28th and last bomber unit to acquire Stratojets, although a 29th unit, the 93rd BW, operated B-47s for just over a year as a necessary prelude to receiving the B-52. The second new wing was the 4080th SRW, which took delivery of the first 'big-wing' RB-57D at Turner AFB, Georgia, at the end of May and which later went on to operate Lockheed's infamous U-2, a type that had been produced in response to the Central Intelligence Agency's requirements and one that was still jealously guarded by this often shadowy organization.

In distinct contrast, the succeeding year was one of considerable change, new units making their débuts, long-established ones disappearing from the scene, operational doctrine being drastically revised, additional bases and subordinate command echelons appearing, a new commanding general being appointed and, last but by no means least, a new headquarters building being fully occupied. It was also a year of head-line-grabbing, record-breaking exploits competing with the advent of new equipment and the retirement of one old favourite, but the major story of 1957 was perhaps Operation 'Power Flite', which earned the 93rd BW the Mackay Trophy. This exercise involved a group of five B-52Bs led by Maj. Gen. Archie J. Old of the 15th AF, who flew aboard the appropriately-named 'Lucky Lady III', accompanied by Lt. Col. James Morris, who had served as the co-pilot aboard 'Lucky Lady II' several years earlier. The flight left Castle AFB on 16 January. Two of the five aircraft were designated as spares, one being forced to leave

45th AD	Loring AFB, Me	42nd BW	69/70/75 BS	B-52D
			42 ARS	KC-97
57th AD	Westover AFB, Ma	99th BW	346/347/348 BS	B-52C
		4050th ARW	26/384 ARS	KC-97
801st AD	Lockbourne AFB, Oh	26th SRW	3/4/10 SRS	RB-47E
			321 ARS	KC-97
		91st SRW	322/323/324 SRS	RB-47E
			91 ARS	KC-97
802nd AD	Schilling AFB, Ks	40th BW	25/44/45 BS	B-47
			40 ARS	KC-97
		310th BW	379/380/381 BS	B-47
			310 ARS	KC-97
817th AD	Portsmouth AFB, NH	100th BW	349/350/351 BS	B-47
			100 ARS	KC-97
818th AD	Lincoln AFB, Ne	98th BW	343/344/345 BS	B-47
			98 ARS	KC-97
		307th BW	370/371/372 BS	B-47
			307 ARS	KC-97
820th AD	Plattsburgh AFB, NY	380th BW	528/529/530 BS	B-47
			380 ARS	KC-97
–	Whiteman AFB, Mo	340th BW	486/487/488 BS	B-47
			340 ARS	KC-97
–	Dow AFB, Me	4060th ARW	71/341 ARS	KC-97

15th Air Force (March AFB, Ca)

12th AD	March AFB, Ca	22nd BW	2/19/33 BS	B-47
			22 ARS	KC-97
		320th BW	441/442/443 BS	B-47
			320 ARS	KC-97
14th AD	Travis AFB, Ca	5th BW	23/31/72 BS	B/RB-36
36th AD	Davis-Monthan AFB, Az	43rd BW	63/64/65 BS	B-47
			43 ARS	KC-97
		303rd BW	358/359/360 BS	B-47
47th AD	Walker AFB, NM	6th BW	24/39/40 BS	B-36
		509th BW	393/715/830 BS	B-47
			509 ARS	KC-97
810th AD	Biggs AFB, Tx	95th BW	334/335/336 BS	B-36
		97th BW	340/341/342 BS	B-47
			97 ARS	KC-97
819th AD	Dyess AFB, Tx	341st BW	10/12/490 BS	B-47
			11 ARS	KC-97
–	Mountain Home AFB, Id	9th BW	1/5/99 BS	B-47
			9 ARS	KC-97
–	Ellsworth AFB, SD	28th BW	77/717/718 BS	RB-36
–	Larson AFB, Wa	71st SRFW	25/82/91 SRS	RF-84F/K
–	Fairchild AFB, Wa	92nd BW	325/326/327 BS	B-36
–	Castle AFB, Ca	93rd BW	328/329/330 BS	B-52B/D
			4017 CCTS	B-52B
			93 ARS	KC-97
–	Altus AFB, Ok	96th BW	337/338/339 BS	B-47
			96 ARS	KC-97
–	Malmstrom AFB, Mt	407th SFW	515/516/517 SFS	F-84F
			407 ARS	KB-29P

the formation when it was unable to take on fuel at the first rendezvous. This B-52 landed safely at Goose Bay, leaving the other four to continue eastwards across the Atlantic to the second refuelling point over Casablanca, where the second spare aircraft, 'City of Turlock', also dropped out, heading north for Brize Norton as planned and becoming the first B-52 to visit the United Kingdom. Three more in-flight refuellings enabled the remaining aircraft to complete the 24,325-

mile non-stop circumnavigation of the world in 45 hours 19 minutes, the only hiccup coming at the end of the flight when fog at Castle necessitated all three aircraft landing at March, instead of only the lead ship as had been intended. Needless to say, General LeMay was on hand to greet his troops, and each member of the three crews received the Distinguished Flying Cross for his part in this remarkable exploit.

Later in the year, following his appointment as Vice Chief of Staff of the USAF, LeMay himself got in on the record-breaking act when he piloted an early production example of the KC-135 from Westover to Buenos Aires, completing the 6,323-mile trip in a little over 13 hours. Two days later, on 13 November, a more direct, 5,204-mile route was taken from Buenos Aires to Washington to set yet another record, LeMay again being the pilot in command. Deliveries of the KC-135 Stratotanker had, in fact, begun on 28 June, Castle AFB in

California being the first base, and the 93rd ARS the first squadron, to acquire this infinitely more capable aircraft. Other early recipients of the KC-135 were the 42nd ARS at Loring and the 99th ARS at Westover, and it was no coincidence that these were all assigned to B-52 wings.

'REFLEX ACTION'

LeMay was still at the helm of SAC when the Command began looking into ways of enhancing its retaliatory posture. Prompted largely by fears about Soviet progress in the area of ICBMs, SAC had for some time been aware of the fact that the day would eventually arrive when it would have little more than 15 minutes' warning of an impending attack. In the face of a surprise onslaught by ICBMs, it was clearly imperative that the degree of combat readiness be increased, and the year 1957 witnessed a succession of tests and trials intended to evaluate just how this heightened alert status might best be

Top: Although it shared the same numerical designation as the earlier Thunderjet, Republic's F-84F was radically improved, hence the choice of a different name – Thunderstreak. These 'Streaks are from the 27th SFW. (Fairchild Republic)

Above: The first true 'high-flyer' to join SAC's rapidly diversifying strategic reconnaissance force was the Martin RB-57D Canberra, which made its début with the 4080th SRW in May 1956. Production of this 'big-wing' B-57 was confined to just twenty airframes.

achieved. In broad terms, SAC's initial plan was to keep roughly one-third of its resources on ground alert, ready for immediate take-off, and in order to establish the best method of achieving this three important tests were conducted.

The first of these, carried out between November 1956 and March 1957, was code-named 'Try Out' and involved two B-47 wings (the 2nd and 308th BWs) of the 38th AD at Hunter AFB, Georgia, along with their associated KC-97 tanker squadrons (2nd and 308th ARS). Experience gained in 'Try Out' proved that the 'one-third alert' was a realistic proposal but also suggested areas where further study was necessary, and SAC duly undertook two further tests as part of the process of preparation. 'Watch Tower', the first, was assigned to the 825th AD at Little Rock AFB, Arkansas, from April until

November 1957, and this Division's two B-47 wings (the 70th SRW and the 384th BW) and one KC-97 squadron (70th ARS) explored some of the difficulties anticipated in manning and organization. Finally there was 'Fresh Approach', a much shorter exercise conducted by the 9th BW at Mountain Home AFB, Idaho, in September, this unit's B-47s and KC-97s providing further proof that ground alert was viable.

Once convinced that it could be made to work satisfactorily, SAC's new commander, Gen. Thomas S. Power, moved ahead aggressively, directing that ground alert duty begin at selected US bases with effect from 1 October. Overseas facilities were not ignored either, changing methods of force deployment permitting alert to be introduced at Sidi Slimane on the same date although, as with the US bases, it was to take

Above: Pictured in company with the Boeing 367-80 prototype, KC-135A 55-3118 'City of Renton' was the forerunner of well over 700 similar aircraft which initially supplanted and eventually replaced the KC-97 series of tankers. As with the B-52, the KC-135 made its début at Castle, where the 93rd Bomb Wing's 93rd Air Refueling Squadron received its first aircraft on 28 June 1957. (Boeing)

Left: A B-47E of the 380th Bomb Wing stands on nuclear alert during a 'Reflex Action' tour of duty at one of the SAC bases in the United Kingdom. (APN)

some time before it was extended to all SAC bases on foreign soil. Briefly, the key to the successful implementation of the system overseas was 'Reflex Action', an entirely new method of deploying SAC bombers and one which held out the promise of a far more effective use of resources. Although the rotational training programme had been a key feature of SAC activity for the last decade, it was by no means ideal, the frequent changeovers being hugely disruptive to the more ordered pattern of operations at home as well as representing a logistical nightmare.

Under 'Reflex Action', selected units supported selected overseas bases, each sending small numbers of aircraft and crews to fulfil alert requirements. This policy was first evaluated at Sidi Slimane with effect from July 1957. The initial test was conducted by four 2nd AF wings, the 2nd, 19th, 308th and 321st BWs, each of which despatched five B-47s to the Moroccan base for short periods of duty. Thereafter, a constantly rotating pattern quickly evolved, aircraft and crews generally spending three weeks at Sidi Slimane before being relieved and permitted to return to their home base, and it soon became apparent that this method was far more conducive to combat readiness – indeed, so successful was this test and the introduction of alert at US bases that 'Reflex Action' soon spread to SAC installations in Britain, Spain, North Africa

Below left: The underground command post in SAC's headquarters complex at Offutt AFB, Omaha, Nebraska. Occupied for the first time in January 1957, it made extensive use of computers to process data relating to force disposition and status, this being presented on the huge display panels which dominated one wall of the control room. (USAF)

and Alaska, and a similar system, entitled 'Air Mail', was put into effect at Andersen AFB, Guam, from the summer of 1958. The last unit to complete a 90-day rotational training tour was the 303rd BW, which returned to Davis-Monthan from Andersen on 4 July 1958; on the other side of the world, the last such tour was made by the 100th BW, which ended its 90-day period of duty at Brize Norton, England, on 1 April 1958.

NEW HEADQUARTERS

Big changes were also evident at the more rarified levels of command, SAC headquarters moving from a motley collection of buildings into a new, S9 million purpose-built control centre during January 1957. The new headquarters took the form of two separate but connected structures, that portion above ground serving as an administrative block. Beneath the surface lay a three-storey command complex, access being gained by tunnel, and the degree of 'hardening' was such that it would be expected to survive all but a direct hit from a high-yield nuclear warhead. Computer technology was everywhere, perhaps the best-known application being the huge display panels which dominated the control room and which provided a constantly updated picture of the disposition and status of SAC's forces throughout the world. Sophisticated communications equipment

Below: In addition to the pure fighter F-84Fs, SAC also acquired sufficient RF-84F Thunderflashes to equip one Strategic Reconnaissance Wing (Fighter), the 71st SRW(F) at Larson AFB, Washington. A small number of RF-84K 'parasites' were also flown by this unit. (Fairchild Republic)

also permitted near-instantaneous contact with the forces at its disposal, with the National Command Authorities in Washington and with other major USAF commands.

Other changes affected organization, the major event of the year perhaps being the acquisition of a fourth numbered Air Force, the 16th. Activated at Torrejon, Spain, in July 1956, the 16th AF spent virtually a year under the control of Headquarters United States Air Forces in Europe (USAFE) before being transferred to SAC on 1 July 1957. Its ultimate brief was to exercise command jurisdiction over SAC forces operating in Spain and, via the subordinate 5th AD, French Morocco, and the transfer to SAC was quickly followed by the first visit of the B-47 to a Spanish base when fifteen aircraft of the 40th BW moved from Greenham Common to Zaragoza for a two-day exercise on 23 July. Eventually, SAC bomber and tanker aircraft became a familiar sight in Spanish skies, the three air bases of Moron, Torrejon and Zaragoza hosting B-47 alert forces engaged on 'Reflex Action' for several years.

With regard to its operational assets, SAC saw a sharp decline in the number of tactical aircraft from around the 3,200 mark to just over 2,700 during 1957. This came about largely through the elimination of fighter elements, the escort mission no longer being valid in view of the planned retire-ment of the lumbering B-36. Of the six units involved – five Strategic Fighter Wings with F-84Fs and one Strategic Reconnaissance Wing (Fighter) with RF-84Fs – four were transferred to Tactical Air Command, the 31st SFW being reassigned on 1 April and the 12th, 27th and 506th SFWs following suit on 1 July (a date which marked the deactivation of both the 71st SRW(F) and the 407th SFW). A few months later, on 25 November, the last KB-29Ps were also eliminated from the inventory when the 27th ARS despatched its final two aircraft for storage, these having mainly been used in support of SAC fighters during the last few years of service.

Little more than a month earlier, in mid-October, the long process of retiring the Stratojet had also begun when the Lockbourne-based 91st SRW started disposing of its RB-47Es prior to this unit's disbandment on 8 November. All was not gloom, however, for June 1957 did mark the appearance of two new aircraft. Mention has already been made of the KC-135, but SAC also received its first U-2 that month, this aircraft going to the 4080th SRW which had moved from Turner to Laughlin in anticipation of receiving Lockheed's notorious high-flyer. By the end of 1957, the 4080th's U-2 complement had risen to around a dozen, serving alongside about twenty examples of the 'big-wing' RB-57D.

Below: If the RF-84F was not exactly a stunning success with SAC, the same claim cannot be made of the infamous Lockheed U-2, which has enjoyed a long and profitable career since it entered service with the 4080th SRW at Laughlin AFB, Texas, in June 1957. When SAC first acquired U-2s, these high-flying aircraft were invariably left in their natural metal finish, as seen here, only switching to black soon after they began performing reconnaissance missions in support of the war in Vietnam. (Lockheed-California)

Sentinels of Peace[*]

THE MISSILE AGE BEGINS

*Motto of the 351st
Strategic Missile Wing

Although Strategic Air Command did not become intimately involved with missiles until late in 1955, it certainly maintained a watching brief over developments in this field through the first half of the decade. As a result, the Command was well aware of the potential of such weapons as both a means of mass destruction and a means of deterrence, and it was well placed to employ these devices. Deployment got under way in the late 1950s when first-generation weapons such as the Northrop Snark and Convair Atlas approached maturity as operational systems with the ability to deliver a nuclear warhead over intercontinental range.

Missile development had begun almost a decade earlier, prompted in large part by German success with the V-2 in the closing stages of the Second World War. In the United States, the Air Research and Development Command (ARDC) was assigned the responsibility for developing and testing guided missiles to a point where operational deployment could take place. The initial thrust of its work was conducted in two broad areas, the intercontinental missile (ICM) and the intercontinental ballistic missile (ICBM). Slightly greater emphasis was given to the former, although work could hardly be said to have progressed at an electrifying pace, limited funding and low priority conspiring to slow down the evolutionary process. The ICBM fared even less well in the early stages, development at one time being halted because of insufficient funds. As a result of this initial tardiness, more than thirteen years were to pass before SAC was able to place its first missile, an Atlas D, on alert at Vandenberg AFB, California, although once wholeheartedly committed to missiles the USA moved in typically aggressive fashion, the pace of progress in the early 1960s perhaps being best indicated by the fact that it took less than five years for the number of ICBMs on alert to outstrip the number of bombers.

THE SNARK MISSILE

In view of the recent controversy over cruise missiles, it is interesting to note that the first weapons to be developed were essentially that. Northrop was awarded a modest research and study contract on 28 March 1946 when SAC was just one week old. In essence, this called for the company to examine the feasibility of both subsonic and supersonic, medium- to long-range (1,500–5,000 nautical miles), surface-to-surface guided missiles or ICMs. Snark was the name given to the subsonic contender, while the supersonic version was known as Boojum, although the latter was cancelled at a fairly early stage of development.

Initially designated SSM-A-3 and later known as the B-62 and SM-62, Snark closely resembled a pilotless aircraft in appearance. The similarities did not stop there, for it was powered by a single Pratt & Whitney J57 turbojet engine capable of propelling it at altitudes of 45,000–50,000ft and at a cruising speed of the order of Mach 0.9. Launch was accomplished from a mobile ground cradle by means of a pair of solid-fuel rocket boosters which were jettisoned once airborne. A single W39 nuclear warhead with a yield in the megaton range was carried in the nose cone, which would separate from the rest of the missile once it was in the vicinity of the target, the warhead thereafter being left to pursue a ballistic trajectory to detonation.

At the time of this weapon's conception the jet fighter was still very much in its infancy, and had Snark been deployed then it seems fair to assume that it would have enjoyed a lengthy operational career. By the time it did become available, however, it had been rather overtaken by events, and SAC's initial enthusiasm was tempered by the fact that the missile was now clearly vulnerable to enemy fighter aircraft. Further doubt was cast by the results of the Snark's test programme, which was plagued by launch failures. Even when it did get airborne successfully, shortcomings with the guidance system meant that the missile's accuracy left a great deal to be desired, and in view of these failings it is hardly surprising that SAC recommended cancellation in late 1958. On this particular occasion, they were overruled, it being felt that the Snark project would be of value in providing SAC with experience of operating missiles and of the procedures to be adopted in bringing later, more capable, weapons on to the inventory.

Preparations for the operational deployment of the Snark began in October 1956 when SAC created the Strategic Missile Site Selection panel, which was charged with defining the requirements for future ICM and ICBM basing, a task which also encompassed the surveying of potential sites. Naturally, target coverage was a key factor in the choice of missile bases and, in the case of Snark, the selection process took into account such matters as range, anticipated target locations and the capability of the weapon. As a result, it was agreed that the first operational Snark missiles be established at Presque Isle AFB in Maine, a decision which was made public on 21 March 1957. Just under two months later, on 17 May, it was decided to conduct Snark training and operational testing from Patrick AFB, Florida. Situated conveniently close to

Below: A test example of the Northrop SM-62 Snark pilotless surface-to-surface intercontinental missile is launched from Patrick, Florida, in the late 1950s. Intended to deliver a single W39 nuclear warhead, Snark employed jettisonable solid-fuel rocket boosters for launch. (Northrop)

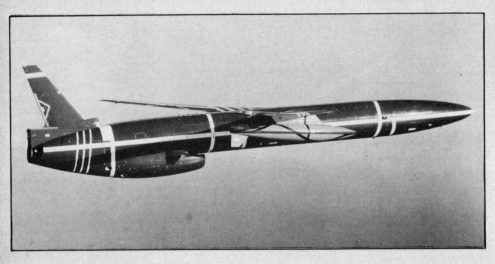

Left: With photographic reference markings clearly visible on the fuselage and with a pair of auxiliary fuel tanks underwing, a Northrop SM-62 Snark test missile flies along the Atlantic Missile Range, which extended eastward from Cape Canaveral and nearby Patrick AFB. (Northrop)

Cape Canaveral, where testing of the Northrop missile was under way, Patrick would be home for the 556th Strategic Missile Squadron (SMS), and this was duly activated on 15 December. The 556th's first successful launch from the Cape took place just over six months later, on 27 June 1958.

By then many of those closely associated with SAC's missile projects were beginning to voice their doubts over the efficacy of the Snark, but plans for its operational deployment moved ahead steadily. On 1 January 1959 the 702nd Strategic Missile Wing (SMW) was activated at Presque Isle, its first subordinate squadron (the Patrick-based 556th SMS) being assigned on 1 April. It was originally intended that the 556th SMS would be one of two squadrons assigned to the 702nd at Presque Isle (the other was to have been the 702nd Missile Maintenance Squadron), and it did actually move north from Patrick on 9 July, a wing detachment henceforth managing Snark launches from the Florida base. However, the 556th's period of tenure at Presque Isle was brief, for it was deactivated on 16 July 1959, and the 702nd SMW's deputy commander for missiles thereafter assumed responsibility for operations and maintenance.

The delivery of Snark missiles to the 702nd predated this event by a couple of months, the first example arriving on 27 May, and by the end of the year SAC had a grand total of thirteen missiles of this type on charge. The process of bringing the 702nd up to its authorized unit establishment of 30 Snarks was painfully slow: indeed, it was not until 18 March 1960 that the first weapon went on alert, and almost a year was to elapse before SAC felt able to

declare the 702nd SMW operational, an event which took place on 28 February 1961. Just under four months later, on 25 June 1961, the 702nd SMW was itself deactivated, a victim of President Kennedy's defence budget message of 28 March which decreed that Snark was 'obsolete and of marginal military value'. The statement vindicated SAC's earlier feelings, and it heralded the end of the Command's association with ICMs.

PROJECT 'ATLAS'

If the ICM can be viewed as being largely a failure, the same claim most certainly cannot be made of the ICBM, which is still very much a part of the SAC inventory, having been subjected to continuous refinement since it first entered service shortly before the end of the 1950s. The evolution of the US ICBM can also be traced back to the late 1940s, Convair having been awarded a research and study contract by the US Army Air Force in April 1946. Financial stringency led to the cancellation of this contract in June 1947, but the residual funds were used by Convair to test a trio of research rockets and to study guidance and nose cone re-entry systems. Effectively, however, the ICBM was accorded a very low priority during this period, and so things remained until 16 January 1951. On that date, and in the light of numerous studies which confirmed that it was now technically feasible to design and produce a long-range rocket capable of delivering the very heavy nuclear weapons then in service, Convair was directed to begin studies for a rocket-powered guided missile with a range of at least 5,500 nautical miles, a speed of at least Mach 6

Right: Barely visible inside its servicing gantry, a development specimen of Convair's Atlas ICBM is prepared for launch at Vandenberg, California. The evolution of this ICBM dates back to the late 1940s, but it was not until President Eisenhower endorsed the project in September 1955 that it really began to make solid progress. (General Dynamics)

over the target, a circular error probability (CEP) not exceeding 1,500ft and the ability to carry a nuclear warhead. Alternative modes, ballistic and glide, were to be explored, the former finding favour in September 1951.

Known by both the Air Force and the company as 'Project Atlas', the work proceeded slowly during the period from 1951 to 1954, largely as a result of its low priority, although technological difficulties concerning the propulsion, guidance and nose cone re-entry systems played a part in inhibiting progress. The size and weight of the warhead was still a major problem, and it was not until late 1953, when the Atomic Energy Commission developed a high-yield, lightweight nuclear device which could, in theory, be easily carried by a missile, that this was overcome. This breakthrough, in conjunction with disturbing reports that the USSR was developing nuclear weapons, and ICBMs to deliver them, proved to be the catalyst which prompted the Air Force to re-evaluate its attitude.

Within a matter of months, a specially convened Strategic Missiles Evaluation Committee, made up of eleven prominent American scientists, had completed a detailed analysis of the US Air Force's ICBM policy as it then stood, recommending in particular that the Air Force establish a special development and management organization to oversee an accelerated programme. This finding was made public in February 1954 and more or less coincided with a Rand Corporation study which indicated that the Atlas rocket could provide the basis for an effective US ICBM force by early in the next decade if the stringent performance stipulations were relaxed, if the level of priority were significantly upgraded and if additional funding were made available.

For Atlas, this proved to be the turning point, for the scale of effort and the amount of cash invested in this project thenceforward rose dramatically, and by the summer of 1954 the Air Research and Development Command (ARDC) had created the Western Development Division (WDD) at Inglewood, California, specifically to manage the Atlas programme; subsequently, in May 1955, this agency also assumed responsibility for Titan, another promising early ICBM proposal and one which was originally viewed as an alternative or back-up for

Far left: Another Snark test round, this time in clean configuration. The Snark project was plagued by problems, which included numerous launch failures and a woefully inadequate guidance system, but, despite these shortcomings, SAC did succeed in bringing the weapon to the status of an operational system with the 702nd Strategic Missile Wing at Presque Isle, Maine. (Northrop)

Left: With the servicing gantry visible in the background, an Atlas sits on the launch pad at Vandenberg at the moment of ignition. The first truly effective ICBM, Atlas attained operational status at Vandenberg shortly before the end of the 1950s, and for a time was the most important weapon of its kind in SAC's arsenal. (General Dynamics)

Atlas. Despite the increased sense of urgency, however, it was to take another year before President Dwight D. Eisenhower put his weight behind the programme. With presidential endorsement – which was forthcoming on 8 September 1955 – Atlas took a major step nearer to becoming an operational system, and no effort was spared to translate this promising project into reality. Two months later, USAF headquarters announced that the ultimate responsibility for the management of the ICBM force would be entrusted to SAC, which would take over from ARDC's WDD as soon as an initial operational capability (IOC) was achieved.

MISSILE DEPLOYMENT

In the meantime, the status of the Titan missile also changed. The Mk. I version of this weapon was earmarked for operational deployment as the second element of the first-generation ICBMs, but it took some considerable time to establish the force mix, which eventually stabilized at thirteen Atlas and six Titan I squadrons, with combined totals of 133 and 54 missiles respectively. Earlier proposed 'mixes' had consisted of 80 Atlas and 40 Titan (December 1955 plan), 40 Atlas and 40 Titan (March 1957) and 83 Atlas and 40 Titan (January 1958), the increased number eventually emplaced being largely prompted by fears concerning Soviet capabilities – fears which began to dominate US defence thinking following the successful orbital flight of the Sputnik I satellite in October 1957. Details of the operational deployment of the Atlas and Titan weapons systems may be found in the accompanying table, along with variants, bases and activation dates, and it can be seen that both types enjoyed only a relatively short front-line career when compared with second-generation ICBMs like Minuteman. Dates quoted do not necessarily refer to periods of operational service: it was common for units to be activated some months in advance of missile emplacement, while the deactivation process was generally predated by the removal of the weapons from their silos.

From SAC's point of view, ICBM planning effectively began in the summer of 1956 and was based on the introduction of both Atlas and Titan. Perhaps the earliest clear signal that the ICBM was moving

nearer to becoming a reality as an operational system came on 1 January 1958, when the 1st Missile Division at Cooke AFB (renamed Vandenberg in October 1958) was transferred from ARDC to SAC, the simultaneous reassignment of the subordinate 704th Strategic Missile Wing (SMW) providing the Command (and, incidentally, the USAF) with its first dedicated missile wing. The 704th's principal function was to serve as a training organization, elements of this wing eventually being intimately associated with Atlas and Titan ICBMs, plus the Jupiter and Thor IRBMs (Intermediate Range Ballistic Missiles). Further preparations which took place in 1958 related to the activation of the first two operational missile wings, the 4320th Strategic Wing (Missile) at F. E. Warren AFB, Wyoming, on 1 February (renumbered as the 706th SMW on 23 February) and the 703rd SMW at Lowry AFB, Colorado, on 25 September. Intended to operate Atlas and Titan I missiles respectively, these units initially reported to the 1st Missile Division, but it was to be some time before they received any weapons.

Three variants of the Atlas, all liquid-fuelled, eventually attained operational status. The D model was the first to enter service, and this employed radio-inertial guidance to deliver a single nuclear warhead, almost certainly a W38 with a yield of 500kt–1Mt. Range was approximately 6,500 nautical miles, but this version was particularly vulnerable since it was stored horizontally, above the ground, in a 'coffin' type

TABLE 3: CONVAIR ATLAS DEPLOYMENT

Unit	Base	Missiles	From	To
576 SMS	Vandenberg, Ca	6 Atlas D; 1 Atlas E; 2 Atlas F	1 Apr 1958	22 Mar 1965
564 SMS	F. E. Warren, Wy	6 Atlas D	1 Jul 1958	1 Sept 1964
565 SMS	F. E. Warren, Wy	9 Atlas D	1 Dec 1958	1 Dec 1964
566 SMS*	Offutt, Ne	9 Atlas D	15 Aug 1959	15 Dec 1964
567 SMS	Fairchild, Wa	10 Atlas E	16 Dec 1959	25 Jun 1965
548 SMS	Forbes, Ks	9 Atlas E	22 Jan 1960	25 Mar 1965
549 SMS†	F. E. Warren, Wy	9 Atlas E	19 Apr 1960	25 Mar 1965
550 SMS	Schilling, Ks	12 Atlas F	22 Jul 1960	25 Jun 1965
551 SMS	Lincoln, Ne	12 Atlas F	24 Oct 1960	25 Jun 1965
577 SMS	Altus, Ok	12 Atlas F	12 Dec 1960	25 Mar 1965
578 SMS	Dyess, Tx	12 Atlas F	25 Jan 1961	25 Mar 1965
579 SMS	Walker, NM	12 Atlas F	14 Mar 1961	25 Mar 1965
556 SMS	Plattsburgh, NY	12 Atlas F	26 Apr 1961	25 Jun 1965

*Unit designation changed to 549 SMS on 1 July 1961; †Unit designation changed to 566 SMS on 1 July 1961.

launcher from which it was elevated to the vertical position for launch. Operational forces eventually numbered just 30 Atlas Ds, distributed among Vandenberg, F. E. Warren and Offutt.

Since it was housed in an unhardened ('soft') storage facility, the Atlas D was clearly unable to cope with nuclear blast, a failing which was to some extent addressed by the Atlas E, 29 examples of which were stationed at Vandenberg, Fairchild, Forbes and F. E. Warren. Storage of the E model was based upon the use of 'semi-hard', 'coffin' launchers which did at least have the merit of providing a measure of protection in the event of a pre-emptive strike. Once the decision to launch the missile had been taken, however, it was necessary to elevate the weapon to the vertical position for firing and it was obviously at risk during this phase of preparation. The Atlas E also employed an all-inertial guidance system, improved and more powerful engines and, in most cases, a larger warhead, the last almost certainly being of the W49 type.

The final Atlas model was the F, which, unlike its predecessors, could be stored in a fully-fuelled state. This reduced the reaction time by a significant margin, while the degree of vulnerability to a first strike or counter-strike was further reduced by emplacing the missile in a hardened, silo-lift launcher. In these facilities – a variation of which, incidentally, was also adopted for the Titan I – the missile was kept underground in a vertical position and only brought to the surface when launch was imminent. All-inertial guidance and a W49 warhead were inherited from the Atlas E, but the final version did feature slightly more powerful engines and it duly became the most numerous model, 74 examples ultimately being distributed among seven bases extending from Vandenberg on the west coast through the heartland of America to Plattsburgh in the east.

ICBM TECHNOLOGY PROGRESSES
Titan I came slightly later, deployment being effected at the beginning of the 1960s. To some extent, this missile provided evidence of the rapid strides being made in ICBM technology in that it was a two-stage, liquid-fuelled missile, the first stage developing some 300,000lb of thrust and the second about 80,000lb. Guidance was

accomplished by a combination of radio and inertial systems, while range was markedly reduced but still impressive, at approximately 5,500 nautical miles. The warhead was, in most instances, the familiar W49 type, although some sources indicate that the W38 was also used, these devices between them offering yields in the 500kt-1Mt range. Regardless of warhead, the 54 Titan I missiles eventually emplaced were distributed across a total of five bases, all of which were situated in the western half of the USA.

If any single event may be said to have signalled the arrival of the ICBM as a weapon of mass destruction, it was probably 'Desert Heat', the code-name assigned to the successful launch of an Atlas D from Vandenberg on 9 September 1959. Conducted by personnel of the 1st Missile Division's 576th SMS, the Atlas travelled some 4,300 miles down the Pacific Missile Range and reached a maximum speed of 16,000mph during the course of its brief flight. Those most closely associated with the programme were understandably jubilant at this achievement, while SAC's commander-in-chief, General Power, expressed his immense satisfaction when he described the launch as a 'tremendous milestone', adding in the same statement that Atlas could now be considered operational. The remark was, perhaps, a little premature, for it was not until 31 October that the first Atlas D was placed on alert at Vandenberg, five more missiles entering the SAC inventory by the end of the year.

Between then and late December 1962 SAC's Atlas and Titan I force was progressively brought to full operational status, but progress was at first very slow, only twelve Atlas Ds being in service by the end of 1960. The beginning of the end for these first-generation weapons was heralded at Malmstrom AFB, Montana, in November 1962 when the first Minuteman ICBMs were declared operational. Just a few months later, in May 1963, it was decided to begin phasing out both the Atlas and Titan I. Initial planning called for all Atlas Ds to be removed from alert duty by the end of FY (Fiscal Year) 1965; Atlas E would follow in FY67, with Titan I disappearing from SAC's line-up in FY68. In the event, this plan was substantially reviewed within days of the first Atlas D being removed from alert on

TABLE 4: MARTIN TITAN I DEPLOYMENT				
Unit	Base	Missiles	From	To
848 SMS*	Lowry, Co	9 Titan I	1 Feb 1960	25 Jun 1965
849 SMS†	Lowry, Co	9 Titan I	29 Feb 1960	25 Jun 1965
850 SMS	Ellsworth, SD	9 Titan I	22 Jun 1960	25 Mar 1965
851 SMS	Beale, Ca	9 Titan I	25 Aug 1960	25 Mar 1965
568 SMS	Larson, Wa	9 Titan I	24 Oct 1960	25 Mar 1965
569 SMS	Mountain Home, Id	9 Titan I	12 Dec 1960	25 Jun 1965

*Unit designation changed to 724 SMS on 1 July 1961; †Unit designation changed to 725 SMS on 1 July 1961.

1 May 1964 as Secretary of Defense Robert McNamara revealed that the Atlas E and Titan I would be the subjects of an accelerated withdrawal programme which would result in both weapons leaving SAC by the end of FY65. It was originally intended that Atlas F be retained until FY68, but it was soon added to the revised timetable.

Paradoxically, the USAF's code-name for the retirement of these first-generation weapons was Project 'Added Effort', and this got under way on 1 May 1964 when the 576th SMS took its handful of Atlas Ds off alert; it terminated less than a year later with the 551st SMS at Lincoln, Nebraska, the last Atlas F being consigned to storage on 20 April 1965. Neither weapon was scrapped, the redundant Atlas missiles being despatched to Norton AFB, California, and the Titan Is to Miro Loma Air Force Station, also in California, and both types were later used as launch vehicles for test projects.

Despite the fact that these first-generation missiles were only operational for some five years, and despite their being in many ways unreliable, their importance should not be underestimated. For example, the two ICBMs were instrumental in enabling SAC to develop and perfect maintenance and operational control techniques. Many difficulties still had to be faced and overcome with the second-generation Minuteman and Titan II, but the contribution made by Atlas and Titan I was immense, and the lessons learned in the early stages of development and deployment helped SAC and the US aerospace industry to get later, far more sophisticated weapons 'right'. At the same time, of course, they also provided a significant and timely boost to the United States' deterrent capability, signalling the determination of the nation not to lag behind in this latest and, in many ways, most terrifying manifestation of the 'Cold War'.

Far left: The ultimate Atlas. Progressive development led eventually to the Atlas F, which was a significant improvement in that it could be stored, fully fuelled, in a hardened silo-lift launch facility. As a consequence, reaction time was greatly reduced, and it is hardly surprising that the F model became the most numerous version of Atlas, some 74 missiles being distributed among seven bases throughout the continental USA. (General Dynamics)

Parati Stamus[*]

FROM MINUTEMAN TO PEACEKEEPER

If the first-generation ICBMs were destined to enjoy only a brief front-line career, the same was most certainly not true of their successors, both Minuteman and Titan II being particularly durable weapons systems. Titan II has recently been retired from SAC service, but Minuteman is still very much a part of the contemporary nuclear arsenal, albeit in a form which has been vastly improved when compared with the missiles which were put on alert duty back in the early 1960s.

Quantitatively and qualitatively SAC's most important ICBM for more than two decades, Boeing's Minuteman attained an initial operational capability in November 1962 when the 10th SMS at Malmstrom, Montana, brought the first two of its five flights to alert status; then, as now, each flight had ten missiles, and there were five flights to each squadron. These were the precursors of an eventual total of 1,000 Minutemen, each weapon being emplaced in a hardened silo with the 'missile fields' extending over vast tracts of land in what is often referred to as 'America's granary'. Montana, North and South Dakota, Wyoming and Missouri all host Minuteman-equip-

"We Stand Ready' – motto of the 497th Air Refueling Wing

ped units, the force ultimately stabilizing at some twenty squadrons distributed among four 150-missile and two 200-missile wings.

Authorization to begin work on the system that would eventually evolve into the Minuteman came on the penultimate day of February 1958, when the Department of Defense directed the US Air Force to institute the lengthy design, development and procurement procedures. Boeing was selected as the prime contractor in October of the same year, at which time the principal concern was to obtain a relatively simple but efficient and 'survivable' ICBM at modest cost. The missile gradually took shape over the next couple of years, emerging as a three-stage, solid-fuelled, rocket-powered weapon possessing a maximum range of around 5,500 nautical miles. Although hard data is not readily available, this figure is perhaps a little conservative: range characteristics quoted for the current Minuteman II and Minuteman III vary from 6,080nm to 8,000nm, and it is common knowledge that these much-improved additions to the family can fly considerably further.

Flight-testing research and development copies of the Minuteman began in February 1961, and this phase of the programme seems to have been accomplished with few serious problems, for the initial production LGM-30A Minuteman I was completed by Boeing in April 1961. By then, Malmstrom AFB, Montana, had been selected as the first Minuteman base and this took delivery of its first missile on 23 July. Emplacement in the hardened silos began on 17 August, and the 341st Strategic Missile Wing's (SMW) first weapon went on alert on 26 October, the first 50-missile squadron, the 10th SMS, being declared fully operational in February 1963.

MOBILE MINUTEMAN

Long before that, however, a particularly interesting chapter in the Minuteman saga had come to an unfortunate end. For some time SAC commanders had been of the opinion that the advantages conferred by freedom of movement far outweighed any disadvantages which might accrue from the lack of hardened accommodation, and in the late 1950s there was a proposal to mount a small proportion of the Minuteman force – anything from 50 to 150

missiles – on specially modified railroad cars with a view to deployment between 1961 and 1963. The idea was the subject of a formal submission to the Air Staff by SAC headquarters on 12 February 1959, by which time some slippage in the timetable had occurred, although it was still felt that such a radical system could be operational by January 1963; the commander of SAC, General Thomas S. Power, reinforced this request in early March when he stated that the mobile Minuteman had much to offer at a time 'when the US is missile-limited'. As it transpired, the Kennedy administration signalled the end of the mobile Minuteman in the defence statement of March 1961, but it was not until 7 December that Secretary of Defense Robert McNamara announced its formal cancellation (those with a sense of history probably not overlooking the fact that this particular date also marked the twentieth anniversary of the Japanese attack on Pearl Harbor).

TABLE 5: MINUTEMAN SQUADRONS			
Unit	Wing	Base	Date organized
10 SMS	341 SMW	Malmstrom AFB, Mt	1 Dec 1961
12 SMS	341 SMW	Malmstrom AFB, Mt	1 Mar 1962
66 SMS	44 SMW	Ellsworth AFB, SD	1 Jul 1962
67 SMS	44 SMW	Ellsworth AFB, SD	1 Aug 1962
68 SMS	44 SMW	Ellsworth AFB, SD	1 Sep 1962
319 SMS	90 SMW	F. E. Warren AFB, Wy	1 Oct 1963
320 SMS	90 SMW	F. E. Warren AFB, Wy	8 Jan 1964
321 SMS	90 SMW	F. E. Warren AFB, Wy	9 Apr 1964
400 SMS	90 SMW	F. E. Warren AFB, Wy	1 Jul 1964
446 SMS	321 SMW	Grand Forks AFB, ND	1 Jul 1965
447 SMS	321 SMW	Grand Forks AFB, ND	1 Feb 1965
448 SMS	321 SMW	Grand Forks AFB, ND	15 Sep 1965
490 SMS	341 SMW	Malmstrom AFB, Mt	1 May 1962
508 SMS	351 SMW	Whiteman AFB, Mo	1 May 1963
509 SMS	351 SMW	Whiteman AFB, Mo	1 Jun 1963
510 SMS	351 SMW	Whiteman AFB, Mo	1 Jul 1963
564 SMS	341 SMW	Malmstrom AFB, Mt	1 Apr 1966
740 SMS	455 SMW*	Minot AFB, ND	1 Nov 1962
741 SMS	455 SMW*	Minot AFB, ND	1 Dec 1962
742 SMS	455 SMW*	Minot AFB, ND	1 Jan 1963

*Discontinued and deactivated 25 June 1968. Squadrons henceforth assigned to 91st SMW at same base.

Far left: Standing on permanent guard duty outside the SAC headquarters building at Offutt AFB, this inert missile is one of the few remaining examples of the first-generation LGM-30A Minuteman I ICBM. Attaining operational status with the 10th Strategic Missile Squadron at Malmstrom AFB, Montana, in November 1962, the LGM-30A was produced in only modest quantities, sufficient being purchased to equip just three 50-missile squadrons. (USAF)

In the meantime, SAC had undertaken a detailed assessment of the viability of this concept, the study phase culminating in a series of tests with a specially configured train. Staged out of Hill AFB, Utah – the home of Air Force Plant 77, where the assembly of the Minuteman missile took place under Boeing's auspices – Operation 'Big Star' demonstrated that the idea was technically feasible. Although six test runs were scheduled, only four were needed to complete the various objectives, the first beginning on 20 June 1960 when the special train rumbled out of Hill. By 27 August, when the fourth test was terminated, operations had been conducted across several hundred miles of track in the western and central USA, during which time considerations such as the suitability of the existing rail network for mobile missile trains, the command, control and communications systems required, the effects of vibration and the manning arrangements had all been examined. SAC thereafter argued loud and long for mobile Minuteman, but the pleas fell on stony ground when the proposal to deploy three squadrons with a total of 150 missiles was deferred in favour of an equivalent number of silo-emplaced weapons at the end of March 1961. From then on, the mobile Minuteman was effectively extinct.

Among the silo-emplaced weapons, the LGM-30A was destined to be produced in only modest quantities, sufficient missiles being procured to equip just three squadrons of the 341st SMW, the 10th, 12th and 490th SMSs. Production then switched to the LGM-30B model, also known as the Minuteman I, and this was manufactured in far greater numbers: eventually, 650 operational missiles equipped a total of thirteen squadrons at four bases, Ellsworth (44th SMW), Minot (455th SMW, later 91st SMW), Whiteman (351st SMW) and F. E. Warren (90th SMW). The differences between the two versions of the Minuteman I were mainly confined to the second-stage engine chamber, that of the LGM-30B being made of titanium instead of steel. The B model was also slightly longer, but both sub-types employed a single one-megaton W59 warhead. The LGM-30F, however, was a true second-generation Minuteman incorporating numerous improvements, and it was the advent of this derivative which signalled the

end of the line for the Minuteman I, the peak strength of 800 LGM-30A/B missiles being maintained for less than a year, between June 1965 and May 1966.

TITAN II

By this time SAC's heavyweight missile, the massive, 327,000lb Martin LGM-25C Titan II, had entered the nuclear arsenal. Like Titan I, this was a two-stage ICBM, but it featured numerous improvements, most notably in its propulsion, storage, guidance system and warhead. Development began shortly before the end of 1959, the planned force being set at six squadrons on 28 March 1961. Each squadron would control nine missiles, giving a total strength of 54, and IOC was attained on 8 June 1963 by the 390th SMW's 570th SMS at Davis-Monthan AFB, Arizona. The deployment of the Titan II was accomplished quite swiftly. All three two-squadron wings attained fully operational status by the end of 1963, other bases with this type of missile having been established at Little Rock AFB, Arkansas (308th SMW), and at McConnell AFB, Kansas (381st SMW).

Above: Each flight of ten Minuteman missiles is controlled by a two-man launch crew, although the 'positive control' doctrine means that it is necessary for a separate launch control centre to verify the launch order, it being physically impossible for a single crew to act independently. In addition, of course, the two officers occupy work stations which are widely separated; since it is necessary for 'key turn' to occur simultaneously, this provides another safeguard by eliminating the possibility of one man precipitating a nuclear holocaust. (USAF)

TABLE 6: TITAN II SQUADRONS			
Unit	Wing	Base	Date organized
373 SMS	308 SMW	Little Rock AFB, Ar	1 Apr 1962
374 SMS	308 SMW	Little Rock AFB, Ar	1 Sep 1962
532 SMS	381 SMW	McConnell AFB, Ks	1 Mar 1962
533 SMS	381 SMW	McConnell AFB, Ks	1 Aug 1962
570 SMS	390 SMW	Davis-Monthan AFB, Az	1 Jan 1962
571 SMS	390 SMW	Davis-Monthan AFB, Az	1 May 1962

Titan II's range is reportedly similar to that of the earlier Titan I (i.e. about 5,500 nautical miles), although there does seem to be a considerable amount of conflicting information, supposedly informed sources mentioning figures which vary from 4,000km (approximately 2,500 miles) to 8,100 nautical miles. The former figure is clearly in error, for reasons which become obvious as soon as one looks at a map – Arizona-based weapons would only be able to strike at targets in Canada or Latin America! Guidance for both models is accomplished by inertial means, the original system having been replaced in the late 1970s and early 1980s, not long before the lengthy process of withdrawal began. Propulsion systems have also been updated, the Titan II's engines being significantly more powerful than those of Titan I, although they are still liquid-fuelled. The two Aerojet LR87-AJ-5 rocket motors which power the first stage generate a combined thrust of no less than 430,000lb, and the second stage's LR91-AJ-5 engine produces a healthy 100,000lb of thrust; between them, they boost Titan II to an impressive 15,000mph at burn-out.

Their emplacement in hardened silos provided the missiles with a much improved likelihood of survival, but the greater complexity of the Titan II system required additional personnel. When compared with the Minuteman, for instance, Titan is labour-intensive, since each silo is linked to an underground launch control facility manned twenty-four hours a day by two officers and two enlisted men; in contrast, the two officers to be found in each Minuteman launch control centre are responsible for a total of ten missiles, and thus the entire Minuteman force of 1,000 weapons actually requires fewer alert-dedicated personnel than the 54 Titan IIs.

Employed in conjunction with the Mk. 6 re-entry vehicle which allegedly offers three-target selection capability and which also incorporates penetration aids, the Titan II's W53 warhead has a yield of 9Mt and is essentially similar to the B53 bomb carried by the B-52 Stratofortress. By the time these words are read, however, Titan II will have been consigned to the realms of history as an operational ICBM. Phasing out the missiles began in October 1982 but was predated by a couple of fuel-related acci-

dents which reduced the number on the inventory from 54 to 52, silos at Rock, Kansas, and Damascus, Arkansas, being rendered useless in explosions which occurred in 1978 and 1980. Formal retirement was initiated by the 390th SMW at Davis-Monthan and the missiles were thenceforth removed at a rate of one per month, the last weapons being due for withdrawal in early 1987.

FORCE MODERNIZATION

If the Titan II no longer features in the SIOP (Single Integrated Operational Plan) or 'war plan', Minuteman II is still very much an integral part of SAC's resources and would

Below: SAC's heavy-weight missile. Now no longer in service, the Martin LGM-25C Titan II was by far the largest ICBM to join SAC, some 54 being emplaced in Arizona, Arkansas and Kansas when at peak strength. Initial operational capability was achieved in June 1963 and phase-out did not begin until October 1982. (USAF)

Left: Titan II was rather more labour-intensive than Minuteman, each of the 54 missile silos having its own launch control centre and a four-man missile combat crew made up of two officers and two enlisted men. Here, a Titan crew runs through one of the many drills which became a routine feature of life underground. (USAF)

Left: This artist's impression conveys more graphically the relationship between the silo which contained the Titan II ICBM and accommodation facilities for the associated missile crew. At right can be seen the missile in its hardened launch facility or 'silo', while at left is the launch control centre. (USAF) Far right: The characteristic smoke ring which generally accompanies the launch of a Boeing Minuteman ICBM from its concrete silo can be seen to the left of the exhaust plume caused by an LGM-30F as it begins its short flight down the Pacific Missile Range from Vandenberg AFB, California. (Boeing)

clearly be employed in any near-term nuclear exchange. Entering its flight-test programme in September 1964, the LGM-30F Minuteman II incorporated numerous improvements in guidance, range, payload and 'hardening' and was the subject of the Minuteman Force Modernization Program, in which all 800 Minuteman Is were eventually to be replaced (although, as it transpired, not necessarily by the LGM-30F variant). The deployment of Minuteman II began with the activation of a new wing, the 321st SMW, at Grand Forks in 1965, and one of the wing's three squadrons, the 447th SMS, was able to claim the distinction of being the first operational Minuteman II unit on 25 April 1966, the other two squadrons following suit by late November of the same year. Even as the 321st was nearing operational status, the 20th and last Minuteman squadron was being formed, this being the 564th SMS, which was assigned to the 341st SMW at Malmstrom. It, too, was destined to be equipped initially with the LGM-30F model, and it eventually became operational on 21 April 1967 – a date which effectively signalled the end of Minuteman deployment since the force now totalled exactly 1,000 missiles.

For the modernization project, extensive modification was necessary to enable existing silos to accommodate the LGM-30F, while associated facilities also required major refurbishment. Work got under way at Whiteman AFB, Missouri, on 7 May 1966, when the 351st SMW's 509th SMS removed its first flight of ten LGM-30Bs from their silos in anticipation of the new equipment, and continued at this base until October 1967 when the 351st regained full operational status. Force modernization resumed at Malmstrom in December, the 341st's other three squadrons all being equipped with the LGM-30A, but progress was by no means as swift as it had been at Whiteman and it was not until late May 1969 that work was completed. By this time, the Minuteman fleet comprised equal numbers of the LGM-30B and LGM-30F, and there followed a hiatus lasting several months before updating resumed with the 91st SMW at Minot AFB, North Dakota. This time, though, the LGM-30B was replaced by the second-generation LGM-30G Minuteman III. However, one other wing did surrender the B for

the F model – the 44th SMW at Ellsworth, which acquired Minuteman IIs made redundant by re-equipping the 321st SMW with LGM-30Gs.

By far the most sophisticated version of Minuteman, the LGM-30G was perhaps most significant in that it introduced SAC to the MIRV (multiple independently targetable re-entry vehicle) concept, it being generally accepted that each Minuteman III missile carries three warheads. Warhead type and yield varies. The original Mk. 12 re-entry vehicle (RV) was married to the 170kt W62 device, while the period from 1980 to 1983 witnessed the progressive introduction of the Mk. 12A RV and the 335kt W78 warhead, all 300 missiles assigned to the 91st and 321st SMWs being reconfigured to accept the latter.

Flight testing the LGM-30G variant began in August 1968, emplacement got under way at Minot on 17 April 1970, and the recipient of the first missile, the 741st SMS, attained operational status just two days before the end of 1970. In addition to MIRV capability, LGM-30G also featured a much improved third stage, a more extensive array of penetration aids, enhanced accuracy (which apparently permits it to engage 'hard' and 'hardened' targets with a greater likelihood of success than that of the LGM-30F) and greater range (supposedly of the order of 8,000 nautical miles).

Preparations for Minuteman III naturally predated the missile's deployment by some months, work on refurbishing the silos at Minot beginning on 12 January 1970, and it was not until 13 December 1971 that the

91st SMW was fully equipped with 150 of the weapons. Concurrently with the final stages of force modernization at Minot, the 321st SMW at Grand Forks also entered the programme, its now-redundant LGM-30Fs finding their way to Ellsworth's 44th SMW as already noted. With re-equipment complete at Grand Forks, attention switched to the 90th SMW at F. E. Warren, which was by then the only wing with the older LGM-30B, the last example of which was removed from alert on 3 September 1974.

The formal programme of Minuteman force modernization was eventually completed on 21 January 1975 with the 90th SMW, having taken no less than nine years to complete, but the process of exchanging missiles had even then not quite come to an end as one squadron of the Malmstrom-based 341st SMW (564th SMS) disposed of the LGM-30F in favour of the LGM-30G between January and July 1970. When this small-scale changeover was complete, SAC exercised control over 550 Minuteman III and 450 Minuteman II ICBMs at six bases. Together with the 54 Titan IIs, this, in theory, gave the Command the ability to deliver no fewer than 2,154 warheads, although in reality the number of warheads was probably slightly smaller since some LGM-30Fs have been configured to carry the Emergency Rocket Communication System (ERCS), a last-ditch package by which some, if not all, of the Minuteman ICBMs can be launched even if ground-based control centres are knocked out. One informed source states that the number of missiles configured as ERCS carriers is eight,

Below: Some idea of the extent of a typical missile field can be gleaned from this map, which depicts the location of the 44th Strategic Missile Wing's 150 Minuteman ICBMs. The 44th is a three-squadron wing with headquarters at Ellsworth AFB, South Dakota, and the letters on the map refer to individual missile flights, each flight of ten ICBMs being controlled by a single Launch Control Center. (USAF)

TABLE 7: MINUTEMAN VARIANTS (SERVICE USE)

Model	Squadrons (SMS)
LGM-30A	10, 12, 490
LGM-30B	66, 67, 68, 319, 320, 321, 400, 508, 509, 510 740, 741, 742
LGM-30F	10, 12, 66, 67, 68, 446, 447, 448, 490, 508, 509, 510, 564
LGM-30G	319, 320, 321, 400, 446, 447, 448, 564, 740, 741, 742

Note: All LGM-30A/B Minuteman I missiles have been retired, while four of the squadrons listed as having operated the LGM-30F Minuteman II – the 446th, 447th, 448th and 564th SMS – are at present equipped with the LGM-30G Minuteman III. Finally, the 400th SMS has disposed of the LGM-30G and the silos made vacant are now being occupied by the MGM-118 Peacekeeper missile.

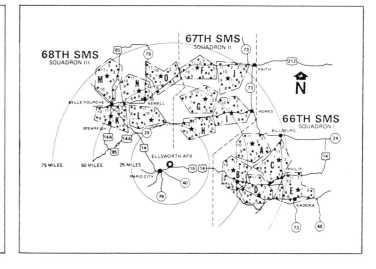

these all being assigned to the 351st SMW at Whiteman.

Updating the Minuteman system did not simply come to an end in 1975, for numerous other initiatives have been undertaken with the objective of increasing 'survivability' and providing greater targeting flexibility. One of the most important of these was Command Data Buffer. A five-year programme which began at F. E. Warren in 1972, and was confined to those elements which operated the Minuteman III, this modification represented a very real advance in that it eliminated the need physically to insert a target tape into each missile; henceforth, electrical means were employed, enabling individual weapons to be reprogrammed in just 25 minutes and the entire fleet of 550 LGM-30Gs in ten hours. At about the same time, the so-called Upgrade Silo Modification programme provided a much greater degree of 'hardness', especially against blast and the effects of electro-magnetic pulse, modernization in this instance being applied to the entire fleet by January 1980. By then a new guidance

system had been evolved for the Minuteman III – the NS-20 all-inertial gimballed package became operational in the summer of 1979 and has since been installed on all examples of this variant – while, as noted earlier, the W78/Mk. 12A warhead/RV was fitted to 300 missiles between 1980 and 1983.

PEACEKEEPER

Updating Minuteman II has been much more modest, although the warhead/RV package has been progressively refined throughout this version's service life; existing LGM-30Fs, for example, employ the W56 Mod. 4/Mk. 11C with a yield of the order of 1.2Mt. The arrival of the MGM-118 Peacekeeper (perhaps better known as MX) is, however, likely to herald a gradual rundown of the Minuteman II, which is now showing signs of age, and the ultimate replacement for the LGM-30F is likely to be the 'Small ICBM', a single-warhead weapon which should enter service in the early 1990s.

Developed over an inordinately long

period, Peacekeeper was designed mainly to close the so-called 'window of vulnerability': by the beginning of the 1970s the Soviet Union had reached the stage where it could perhaps obliterate the United States' own land-based ICBMs in a single pre-emptive strike while using only about 25 per cent of its resources. What was needed was a new weapon, which, in the words of Defense Secretary Caspar Weinberger, would provide the USA with the 'retaliatory capability to inflict on them such damage that they would not make that first strike'. MX was intended to be that weapon, original planning anticipating a method of deploying the missiles which would ensure the survival of a significant retaliatory capability: fundamentally, the idea was to remove any temptation for the USSR to initiate a full-scale nuclear attack by making it quite clear that such a war could never be won (an idea which, incidentally, was never likely to gain much credence, largely by virtue of the existence of the large US fleet of nuclear-powered and nuclear-armed submarines, which were a powerful deterrent in their own right).

SAC, however, was determined to obtain a new ICBM, and set about the long process in November 1971 when it submitted a study stating its requirements. Authorization to proceed with what eventually became known as MX was duly forthcoming, advanced development being initiated in May 1974. The mode of deployment was the subject of extensive study and the cause of considerable expenditure – indeed, it was central to much of the controversy which has surrounded MX, and, together with other considerations such as arms control and the effects of the bases on the environment, eventually prompted Congress to restrict funding for a time in the early 1980s, which of course delayed the missile's operational introduction.

Peacekeeper is intended for use against 'hardened' targets such as missile control facilities, ICBM silos and command centres, payload capability being such that a maximum of twelve re-entry vehicles may be carried by the weapon's bus. However, it now appears that the normal load will comprise ten Mk. 21/W87 RV/warhead pairings, each with a yield in the 300kt range – a combination which was selected to replace the originally specified Mk. 12A/W78 in January 1982. A four-stage missile, Peacekeeper is novel amongst US ICBMs in that it

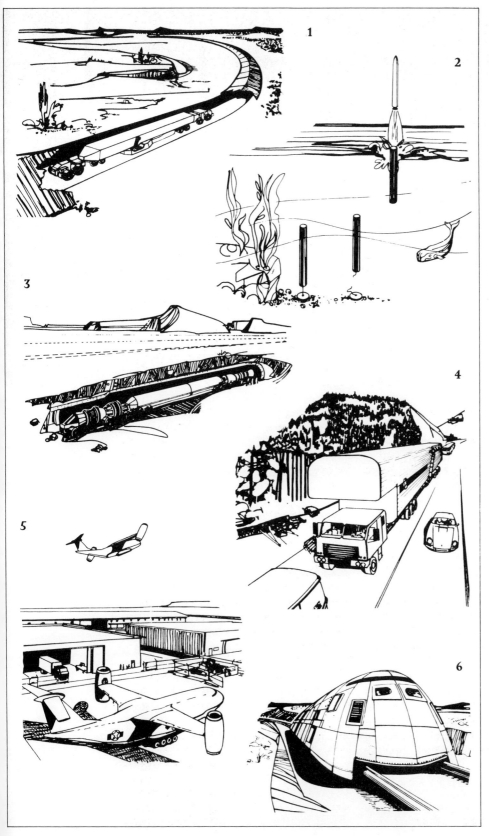

1

2

3

4

5

6

Far left: SAC's newest and most potent ICBM is the MGM-118A Peacekeeper, which began life as MX. After much debate over basing modes, Peacekeeper is now being emplaced in former Minuteman silos of the 400th Strategic Missile Squadron at F. E. Warren AFB and attained initial operational capability in late 1986. The ultimate application of MIRV technology, each Peacekeeper missile can carry as many as ten warheads in the post-boost vehicle. This weapon breaks new ground in that it is the first land-based US ICBM to employ 'cold launch', gas generators being used to propel it from its canister before engine ignition occurs. (USAF)

Left: Many MX basing modes were evaluated, and six of the more original concepts are illustrated. 1. Covered Trench, with randomly travelling missiles penetrating the metallic fabric 'roof'. 2. ORCA, consisting of encapsulated missiles anchored to the sea bed. 3. Shallow Tunnel, with missiles travelling randomly about 5ft beneath ground level. 4. Road Mobile, utilizing scattered launch sites on public roads. 5. 'Grasshopper', comprising about 1,500 VTOL aircraft each carrying one small ICBM. 6. Dedicated Rail Mobile, using a specially built, automated railway system.

employs 'cold launch' techniques, pressure from gas generators being used to eject it from its storage canister; once the missile is clear of the silo, main engine ignition occurs and powered flight begins. Each of the first three stages is solid-fuelled. The fourth and final stage (also referred to as the post-boost vehicle) employs storable liquid fuel and contains the inertial measurement unit which is the heart of the guidance system. A small rocket motor in the shroud or nose cone permits the deployment module to be exposed once in space, and subsequent manoeuvring, accomplished by means of the main axial engine and smaller attitude control motors, enables each of the ten RVs to be released at pre-programmed positions, the RV and its associated warhead thereafter being left to pursue a ballistic path to its designated target. The Peacekeeper reaches altitudes of the order of 700,000ft and has a range possibly exceeding 7,000 nautical miles.

'DENSE PACK'

At least forty different basing concepts were studied before the USAF finally selected the CSB (Closely Spaced Basing) or 'dense pack' system that was ultimately rejected by a Congress which was never convinced by the 'fratricide' argument; instead, existing Minuteman silos which form part of the 90th SMW at F. E. Warren AFB are being modified to take Peacekeeper so as to permit this weapon to attain operational status rather earlier than would otherwise be possible. Initial operational capability with a flight of ten missiles is imminent at the time of writing.

Space does not permit a detailed examination of the alternative basing modes that were considered, but one option which should be mentioned was the Multiple Protective Structure (MPS) selected by the Carter administration in the summer of 1979. In essence, this called for the construction of 200 'race tracks' of about 25 miles' circumference in remote parts of Nevada and Utah. Each track would feature 23 shelters and a single encapsulated missile mounted on a transporter-erector-launcher (TEL) vehicle; the use of decoys would make it virtually impossible for the enemy to establish just which shelter contained a weapon, whilst the degree of mobility inherent in the system would further compound the problem of targeting. Any pre-emptive strike would, therefore, have to be able to guarantee the destruction of all 4,600 shelters – a tall order.

In the event, MPS was quietly abandoned, the succeeding Reagan administration opting in November 1982 for 'dense pack', which would apparently compensate for greater Soviet ICBM accuracy by using 'superhardness' and proximity to overcome the threat. CSB envisaged the deployment of 100 Peacekeeper missiles in a single field, with no more than 1,800ft between the silos. Coupled with 'superhardening' measures which would enable the silos to survive over-pressures of up to 5,000psi, a separation of that order would prevent a single incoming warhead from destroying more than one Peacekeeper whilst also maximizing the so-called 'fratricide' effect, the phenomenon of detonating Soviet warheads deflecting or destroying other warheads targeted on the same complex. That, at least, was the theory, and while the USAF was of the opinion that from 50 to 70 per cent of the Peacekeeper force would survive there were others who held markedly differing views. Some of the sceptics occupied senior positions in Congress and were in large part responsible for controlling the purse strings, and so it was hardly surprising that CSB failed to gain approval.

These arguments notwithstanding, Peacekeeper is an important addition to the US nuclear arsenal, as also will be the proposed 'Small ICBM', the full-scale development of which is expected to begin during the course of FY87 with deployment following in the early 1990s. Recent studies point to a three-stage weapon in the 25,000–35,000lb weight class and possessing the ability to deliver a single warhead over a range of about 7,000–8,000 miles. Numerous ways of deploying the missile appear to exist, these varying from a modification of 'dense pack' to mobile armoured launchers, but perhaps the biggest stumbling block concerns a violation of existing arms agreements, because SALT II restricts the number of launchers to 2,250. However, since the USA recently exceeded the permitted number of cruise missile-carrying B-52s, the problem may well prove not to be insurmountable, especially in view of the fact that SALT II was never formally ratified by the USA in the first place.

Willing, Able, Ready*

DISPERSING THE FORCE

By the beginning of 1958 Strategic Air Command had clearly come a long way. Old and obsolescent bomber aircraft like the B-29 and B-50 had been eliminated from the operational inventory, their places taken by hundreds of sleek and shiny B-47s and B-52s with the ability to deliver nuclear weapons to virtually any point on the globe. Looking to the future, Convair's delta-winged, Mach 2 B-58 Hustler was also very firmly in prospect, early flight testing having demonstrated an exhilarating performance. About the only cloud on the horizon concerned a Convair product of a much earlier generation, namely the ten-engined (six piston, four turbojet) B-36, which was still operational in four SAC wings. Even here, though, re-equipment was imminent: two of the four units concerned, the 5th and 7th BWs, disposed of the B-36 in favour of the B-52 during the course of 1958, while the other two, the 72nd and 95th BWs, had both begun the process of phase-out by the end of the year, again preparatory to receiving

Boeing Stratofortresses. Aerial refuelling had made great strides and was now a routine feature of day-to-day operations. The several hundred KC-97s on strength were being joined by a rapidly growing number of jet-powered KC-135s as 1958 progressed, while developments in missiles augured well for the future.

If the Command was in good shape in terms of equipment, there were nevertheless some areas where improvement was necessary – indeed vital if the primary mission, deterrence, were to continue effectively. In 1958, of course, the threat posed by Soviet ICBMs was practically non-existent, but it was becoming clear that the USSR was fast approaching the point at which it *could* deliver nuclear warheads over vast distances by such means; it was equally clear that SAC would, in the very near future, no longer be able to enjoy the security offered by distance, if only by virtue of the fact that warning time would inevitably be greatly diminished when (it was no

*Motto of the 43rd Bomb Wing

Below: In addition to a huge fleet of B-47s and B-52s, SAC was in 1958 anxiously awaiting the availability of Convair's B-58 Hustler, the first supersonic bomber to enter service in the West. However, production was curtailed and only two wings ever utilized the type, which was withdrawn in 1969–70 after barely a decade of service. The aircraft shown here began life as part of the development batch and was subsequently modified to serve as a TB-58A trainer. (General Dynamics)

longer simply a question of 'if') the Soviet Union succeeded in deploying its first ICBM.

DISPERSAL

In the immediate past, SAC had gone through a period of massive expansion and this, in turn, had led to what might be called overcrowding at several air bases, some of which, for example, were home to two fully fledged Medium Bomb Wings whose total resources amounted to more than 90 B-47s and 40 KC-97s. These facilities, to be sure, were well able to support operations of such magnitude in the more normal course of events, but were the USSR to mount a surprise ICBM attack it was obvious that time would not permit more than a fraction of the force to be launched on a retaliatory strike. SAC's response to this challenge was to initiate the so-called 'dispersal' programme, whereby the huge concentrations of bomber and tanker aircraft would be broken up and redistributed among a large number of other bases, thus, at a stroke, compounding Soviet targeting problems while at the same time enabling the Command to put more bomber and tanker resources in the air in the fifteen minutes or so that it would have at its disposal in the event of a surprise missile attack. Dispersal was accomplished over a period of several years and took a variety of forms. Some KC-97 squadrons, for example, were reassigned to bases located in the north, more or less beneath the routes that SAC bombers would take if called upon to attack. B-47 units, on the other hand, were generally left in situ, it being felt that dispersal could best be achieved by the progressive phasing out of the aircraft, although the limited availability of bomber bases, most of which were evidently earmarked for the ever-expanding B-52 fleet, was probably a factor.

At the beginning of 1958 several variants of the Stratofortress were already well established in SAC service. The original B-52B model had been joined by the B-52C, B-52D and B-52E, and the last of the 'tall-tailed' derivatives, the B-52F, was on the brink of joining the Command. Even more capable versions of the aircraft were in prospect: the short-finned B-52G was to make its maiden flight in the late summer of 1958, with delivery to operational units commencing in February 1959, and further off in the future lay the ultimate 'Buff', the turbofan-powered B-52H, generally referred to by SAC aircrews as 'the Cadillac'.

Dispersing the B-52s began in 1958, the same year in which the B-52 force was set at a total of 42 squadrons, each with a nominal unit establishment of fifteen aircraft. Had the ICBM threat not emerged when it did, it seems reasonable to assume that SAC would simply have followed existing patterns of deployment, organizing a total of fourteen three-squadron wings and assigning each of these wings to a different airfield; thus a typical B-52 base would have been expected to support 45 bombers and an associated Heavy Air Refueling Squadron with twenty KC-135 Stratotankers. Although dispersal intervened, it is worth noting that SAC's original intention to equip just fourteen Bomb Wings with this type was to some extent reflected by the eventual distribution of the B-52 fleet.

As it transpired, the three-squadron-per-wing practice was partly followed, all the first half-a-dozen wings which acquired the B-52 being organized along these lines; in order of conversion, these were the 93rd BW at Castle, the 42nd at Loring, the 99th at Westover, the 92nd at Fairchild, the 28th at Ellsworth and the 6th at Walker, transition being effected between June 1955 and early 1958. In most cases the period of operation as a full-sized, 45-aircraft wing was brief, subordinate squadrons and aircraft being removed and reassigned to new bases as the programme of dispersal took hold. With the sole exception of the 93rd BW, which had utilized the B-47 for about eighteen months to obtain jet experience in anticipation of serving as the B-52 training unit, all these units had formerly been equipped with Convair's lumbering but stately B-36.

With dispersal now an active programme, the next three Bomb Wings to convert were all initially organized as two-squadron units with a total of 30 B-52s, but in all three cases bomber assets were eventually halved, each wing losing one squadron and fifteen aircraft. In order of re-equipment, these were the 11th BW at Altus, the 7th BW at Carswell and the 5th BW at Travis, the process of transition from the B-36 being accomplished in 1958–59. The final five of the original fourteen Bomb Wings all evolved into single-squadron wings with a complement of fifteen

Right: The final 'tall-tailed' Stratofortress was the B-52F, some 99 aircraft of this sub-type being completed at Seattle and Wichita before production switched to the more capable B-52G. Entering service in 1958, the B-52F was the first version of Boeing's heavyweight to see combat in South-East Asia. (B.M. Service)

bombers, re-equipment being undertaken between 1959 and 1962. The first two, the 72nd BW at Ramey and the 95th BW at Biggs, relinquished the B-36, while the final three, the 97th at Blytheville, the 379th at Wurtsmith and the 19th at Homestead, had all previously operated B-47s.

THE 'STRAT WINGS'

The reductions in the size of the Bomb Wings detailed above constituted just one aspect of dispersal, but perhaps the major manifestation arose from the physical process of relocation. Indeed, by the time this programme was completed in the early 1960s, B-52s were to be found at some 37 air bases throughout the length and breadth of the United States as well as at one facility in Puerto Rico. A key aspect of this realignment concerned the establishment of 22 Strategic Wings between 1957 and 1959, these being organized specifically to exer-

Above: An early production B-52E tops up its tanks from a KC-135A somewhere over the United States. (USAF)

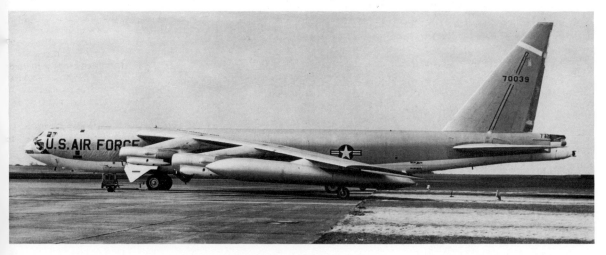

cise operational and administrative control over those squadrons which were physically detached from their former parent Bomb Wings and shifted to new quarters. Activating the so-called 'Strat Wings' began in 1957 when the 4123rd SW was established at Clinton-Sherman AFB, Oklahoma. A further thirteen such units were created in 1958, although only three had been equipped or begun to equip with the B-52 by the end of the year; the activation of the final eight followed in 1959, but for some – most notably the 4133rd SW at Grand Forks AFB, North Dakota – the interval between their formation and the actual allocation of equipment lasted more than two years.

Organization seems to have been virtually uniform, a typical Strategic Wing comprising one fifteen-aircraft Bomb Squadron equipped with the B-52 and one Heavy Air Refuelling Squadron with either ten or fifteen KC-135s. The only units which did not conform to this rule were those at Amarillo (4128th SW), Eglin (4135th SW), Glasgow (4141st SW) and Kincheloe (4239th SW), although three of these bases did acquire their own tanker resources within a matter of months of the 1963 deactivation and reactivation exercise which resulted in the elimination of the Strategic Wings and their replacement by historically significant Bomb Wings. Eglin, however, never hosted KC-135s, neither the 4135th SW nor the 39th BW ever controlling a tanker squadron.

To provide a clearer appreciation of the mechanics involved in dispersal it might be instructive to examine one of the units concerned in greater detail, and the Travis-based 5th BW is representative. Operating the B-36 until the summer of 1958, it controlled three subordinate Bomb Squadrons, these being the 23rd, 31st and 72nd BSs. The last-mentioned squadron was the first to depart, being physically detached from Wing control on 1 July 1958 when it moved to new quarters at Mather AFB, California. Henceforth, it reported to the 4134th Strategic Wing, and it was eventually equipped with a fleet of fifteen B-52Fs in October of the same year, tankers being added to the 4134th's inventory on 1 March 1959 when the 904th ARS was activated to operate the KC-135A. The 23rd and 31st BSs now constituted the bomber elements of the 5th BW, which was initially reorganized as a two-squadron wing, taking delivery of its first B-52G in February 1959. A further reduction in size occurred at the beginning of October 1959 when the 31st BS was reassigned to the control of the 4126th SW at Beale AFB, California, although, as it turned out, it did not actually move to its new quarters until 18 January 1960. In the meantime, bomber operations continued from Travis, the 31st BS being attached to the 5th BW throughout this brief interval. Beale also acquired KC-135s, the 903rd ARS being established on 1 April 1959. Following the departure of the 31st BS, the 5th BW was left in control of one Bomb Squadron with B-52Gs (the 23rd BS) and one Heavy Air Refueling Squadron with KC-135As (the 916th ARS), the latter having been activated as recently as 1 September 1959.

Similar realignment exercises were undertaken by most of the original fourteen wings, and by the beginning of 1963 B-52 dispersal was virtually complete, details of force composition appearing in the accompanying table. In mid-September of that year the deactivation of single squadrons within the 6th Strategic Aerospace Wing (39th BS) and the 93rd Bomb Wing (330th BS) made available sufficient aircraft to permit B-52Bs to be assigned to the 2nd BS, 22nd BW, at March, California, and B-52Es to the 337th BS, 96th SAW, at Dyess, Texas. This effectively signalled the successful completion of dispersal: SAC's Stratofortress fleet was now widely scattered and, as a result, infinitely more 'survivable' and responsive to 'the threat'.

'ALERT' OPERATIONS

In the meantime SAC was also moving ahead with a number of measures designed to facilitate the recently introduced 'one-third' alert programme. The implications of this new concept of operations were wideranging and had perhaps the most profound effect on those wings which were equipped with the B-47, a type which was not destined to be subjected to the same methods of dispersal as those employed for the B-52. Since 'alert' operations logically fell into a four-cycle pattern comprising ground alert, flight planning, flying and a day off, it was fairly obvious that the existing arrangements would need a certain amount of modification if this were to be introduced throughout the medium bomber force. Tests like 'Try Out' and 'Fresh Approach' had helped to pinpoint those areas where urgent change was needed, and further study of the resulting data culminated in some upheaval during the last few months of 1958 when reorganization began.

One of the key elements of the programme concerned the activation of a fourth Bomb Squadron within most of the B-47 wings. However, the reorganization was by no means confined to tactical elements, those responsible for maintenance also experiencing drastic change as part of the need to centralize such functions; for example, deputy commanders for operations and maintenance were appointed to assist wing commanders. Little Rock, Arkansas, and Lincoln in Nebraska were selected to introduce the new arrangements on 1 September 1958. Subsequently, it was intended to reorganize one base in

Unit	Bomb Sqns.	Base	Tanker Sqn.
5 BW	23 BS	Travis, Ca	916 ARS
6 SAW	24/39/40 BS	Walker, NM	6 ARS
7 BW	9 BS	Carswell, Tx	–
11 SAW	26 BS	Altus, Ok	96 ARS
19 BW	28 BS	Homestead, Fl	407 ARS
28 BW	77 BS	Ellsworth, SD	28 ARS
42 BW	69/70 BS	Loring, Me	42 ARS
72 BW	60 BS	Ramey, PR	915 ARS
92 SAW	325 BS	Fairchild, Wa	92 ARS
93 BW	328/329/330 BS	Castle, Ca	93/924 ARS
95 BW	334 BS	Biggs, Tx	917 ARS
97 BW	340 BS	Blytheville, Ar	914 ARS
99 BW	346/348 BS	Westover, Ma	–
379 BW	524 BS	Wurtsmith, Mi	920 ARS
4038 SW	341 BS	Dow, Me	71 ARS
4039 SW	75 BS	Griffiss, NY	41 ARS
4042 SW	526 BS	K. I. Sawyer, Mi	46 ARS
4043 SW	42 BS	Wright-Patterson, Oh	922 ARS
4047 SW	347 BS	McCoy, Fl	306 ARS
4123 SW	98 BS	Clinton-Sherman, Ok	902 ARS
4126 SW	31 BS	Beale, Ca	903 ARS
4128 SW	718 BS	Amarillo, Tx	–
4130 SW	335 BS	Bergstrom, Tx	910 ARS
4133 SW	30 BS	Grand Forks, ND	905 ARS
4134 SW	72 BS	Mather, Ca	904 ARS
4135 SW	301 BS	Eglin, Fl	–
4136 SW	525 BS	Minot, ND	906 ARS
4137 SW	342 BS	Robins, Ga	912 ARS
4138 SW	336 BS	Turner, Ga	919 ARS
4141 SW	326 BS	Glasgow, Mt	–
4170 SW	327 BS	Larson, Wa	43 ARS
4228 SW	492 BS	Columbus, Ms	901 ARS
4238 SW	436 BS	Barksdale, La	913 ARS
4239 SW	93 BS	Kincheloe, Mi	–
4241 SW	73 BS	Seymour-Johnson, NC	911 ARS
4245 SW	717 BS	Sheppard, Tx	900 ARS

each of the three numbered air forces on the first day of each month, and by the end of the year eight more B-47 bases had followed suit. Work on this project continued until well into 1959, Plattsburgh being the last Stratojet base to change over. B-52 wings were also involved although the programme was not accomplished in quite the same way, for, with dispersal fast becoming a reality, there was no need to activate a fourth tactical squadron.

'Alert' methods at bases overseas were also drastically revamped. Prompted by the desire to maintain aircraft on alert at a number of these bases, 'Reflex Action' had

Far left: As an active programme, B-52 'dispersal' was completed in about 1961 when the 4133rd Strategic Wing at Grand Forks, North Dakota, took delivery of the B-52H, and one of their aircraft is seen here at RAF Greenham Common after completing a training flight in the early 1960s. (APN)

begun at Sidi Slimane in the summer of 1957 and was progressively expanded during 1958. Wing-strength rotational training had not quite come to an end, however, and three B-47 wings completed 90-day deployments in the first half of 1958, two of these units (the 341st and the 303rd BWs) carrying out their tours of duty at Andersen AFB, Guam, between January and July and the other, the 100th BW, spending the first three months of the year at RAF Brize Norton, England. Nevertheless, 'Reflex'-dedicated B-47 bomber task forces had been assembled at Fairford and Greenham Common when the new year was just seven days old, with aircraft drawn from a total of five wings; Brize Norton duly introduced this concept within days of the departure of the 100th BW and Mildenhall followed suit in July. 'Reflex' was not, of course, confined to SAC bases in Great Britain, and other facilities which supported this method of force dispersal between 1958 and 1965 were located in Alaska, Morocco and Spain, while an essentially similar operation, code-named 'Air Mail', was conducted at Andersen starting in the summer of 1958.

The introduction of the new doctrine of ground alert was inevitably accompanied by an urgent need for additional combat-rated personnel. To satisfy this requirement, SAC elected to divert a pair of reconnaissance-dedicated units to crew training, an action which had little impact on overall combat readiness since the Command was then suffering from an embarrassment of riches in terms of its photo-reconnaissance capability, having procured rather more RB-47Es than it really needed. This surplus permitted the two RB-47E wings selected to fulfil this task to be switched very quickly: the 90th SRW at Forbes AFB, Kansas, took up its new role from 15 May 1958, while the Little Rock-based 70th SRW followed suit on 15 June. Two weeks later SAC gained responsibility for all B-47 combat crew training when Air Training Command's 3520th CCTW was reassigned, the transfer being effected on 1 July and resulting in a change of designation of the McConnell-based unit to the 4347th CCTW. Thus, in the space of barely six weeks, the number of B-47s assigned to training functions was exactly doubled, rising to 180.

Initiatives designed to enhance alert posture were by no means confined to the bomber force. Tankers were in many ways a vital adjunct to SAC's new philosophy, and there was clearly an urgent need for more aircrews to man these aircraft since the Air Refueling Squadrons were also deeply committed to the ground alert programme. The responsibility for training KC-135 crews was then, as now, mainly the preserve of the 93rd BW at Castle. The flow of personnel from this source was generally sufficient to meet the demand but the position with the KC-97 was rather less satisfactory. Accordingly, on 1 July, SAC set about increasing its capability in this area, organizing the 4397th Air Refueling Wing at Randolph AFB, Texas, and building it up to its planned strength of 40 KC-97s, a level which was maintained until its deactivation in 1962 when the phase-out of the 'Strat' was being accelerated.

Even as SAC was taking measures aimed at ensuring that the 'alert' requirements would be satisfied, the United States became embroiled in the latest manifestations of world tension, back-to-back crises on opposite sides of the globe necessitating vigorous and visible action by various elements of the American military. Naturally, SAC was heavily involved in the shows of force staged at this time. The first potential flash-point – and one which has been a persistent thorn in the side of the USA in recent times – was the Lebanon. A high-level request for assistance arose from fears that the country's independence was being threatened by the United Arab Republic, and overt military action occurred on 15 July 1958 when nearly 2,000 Marines waded ashore at Beirut while tactical aircraft from 6th Fleet carriers furnished air cover for the task force. Less obvious was the fact that SAC very quickly came to a heightened state of alert, the preparation of well over 1,000 aircraft for the possibility of war being one of several measures instigated by President Eisenhower at the height of the crisis. With the immediate threat averted, SAC reverted to the more usual levels of preparedness a few days later, but elements of the Command were again alerted in late August when Chinese artillery began bombarding the Kinmen Islands. As before, carrier-borne air power – this time from the 7th Fleet – was quick to respond, whilst SAC's reactions included boosting the strength of 'Air Mail' forces at Andersen and alerting a

number of US-based bomb wings for the possibility of hurried deployment to the Western Pacific. Once again, though, the crisis passed safely and a state of normality soon returned.

AIRBORNE ALERT
While the problems in Taiwan continued to make news, the testing of an even more radical concept of 'alert' operations was under way, the task of evaluation being assigned to the 42nd Bomb Wing at Loring AFB, Maine. Consisting of three squadrons equipped with the B-52D, the 42nd was probably the best qualified wing to undertake this duty, having gained a considerable amount of experience since converting to the Stratofortress in 1956. The test project was given the code name 'Head Start I' and, conducted between 15 September and 15 December, was intended to establish whether airborne alert was a feasible proposition. As had been the case with the ground alert tests, 'Head Start I' eventually proved to be the forerunner of operational implementation, but testing was destined to continue for some time, with about 6,000 sorties flown in 1959–60. Throughout that

period, fully armed B-52s were kept aloft 24 hours a day, ready to proceed to their targets in the event of the emergency war order being transmitted, and airborne alert became a routine facet of SAC operations in the early 1960s when 'Cold War' tension rose to unprecedented levels as a result of the Berlin and Cuban crises. Although there were almost certainly increases in the number of aircraft engaged in airborne alert at times of crisis, in the more normal course of events this was a relatively low-key operation, seldom involving more than a dozen or so B-52s, although even that modest number of aircraft possessed the ability to inflict tremendous damage. Perhaps the greatest value of airborne alert, though, was the fact that it clearly signalled US determination not to be taken by surprise, while it was always evident that the number of aircraft engaged in this activity could very quickly be increased.

If 1958 can best be remembered as the year in which far-reaching changes were made to 'alert' doctrine, 1959 was no less significant. Dispersal efforts, naturally, were well to the fore, roughly half the newly created Strategic Wings being either fully or

Above: With alert a regular feature of SAC's activities, there came an increased need for combat-ready crews to man both bomber and tanker aircraft. The Command acted in typically aggressive fashion to address this requirement, greatly expanding B-47 crew training facilities and also organizing a KC-97 training unit at Randolph AFB, Texas. In addition to providing in-flight refuelling support for its own bombers. SAC occassionally furnished fuel to aircraft of other commands, typified in this photograph of a development F-101A Voodoo in contact with a SAC KC-97F. (USAF)

partly equipped before the year was out. These changes had some impact on overall organization, of course, and evidence of this was provided by the establishment of several new air divisions to facilitate the command and control of those units which occupied tenant status at other air bases.

Routine training missions provided incontrovertible evidence of major changes in operating technique, the ever more sophisticated network of Soviet defences forcing SAC to reappraise the methods it would have to employ in order to penetrate Russian air space. With new and potentially lethal jet fighters entering the Soviet arsenal in considerable numbers, and with surface-to-air missiles beginning to pose a serious threat, it was clear that bombers could no longer rely on extreme altitude to render them immune from interception. Henceforth, the only way to attack would be at low level, and this duly began to feature in training sorties in 1959 when SAC and the Federal Aviation Agency got together to select a number of areas where regular low-level flying could be undertaken without disrupting civilian operations and with the

minimum of noise nuisance. An initial batch of seven routes, each about 20 miles wide and up to 500 miles long, came into use in 1959. These were at first known as 'Oil Burner', although the name was later changed to the far less emotive 'Olive Branch', and from now on most training missions would feature a low-level sector during which crews became familiar with the very different demands of flight at altitudes of about 400–500ft. Needless to say, accidents occurred, a succession of fatigue-induced failures having disastrous results for a number of B-47s. Even the immensely strong B-52 was not immune to the sometimes devastating effects of severe turbulence, as several crews learned to their cost.

PEAK STRENGTH

The year 1959 may also be said to have represented the high-water mark for SAC, inasmuch as it attained its peak strength in terms of numbers of tactical aircraft in December that year, when well over 3,000 were on charge. Bombers naturally predominated, the 1,366-strong B-47 fleet still

Below: In addition to ground alert, SAC also explored airborne alert procedures, first testing this concept in late 1958 when the Loring-based 42nd BW conducted a three-month evaluation. By the beginning of the 1960s, airborne alert was a routine feature of B-52 operations but the number of aircraft involved was usually modest, rising occasionally in response to major crises such as that which arose when Soviet medium-range missiles were deployed to Cuba. Eventually, following a series of accidents, airborne alert was abandoned. (Boeing)

occupying a position of clear numerical supremacy although the B-52 force was expanding steadily, having reached 488. Gone at last was the 'aluminium overcast', its ten-year tenure coming to an end on 12 February when the 95th BW at Biggs despatched its last B-36J (coincidentally, the final example of the Convair machine to be built) to a permanent resting place at Fort Worth. SAC now had a bomber force that was entirely jet-powered.

Reconnaissance aircraft numbered just over 200. Boeing's Stratojet was, again, the most numerous single type, an assorted fleet of 174 RB-47Es, RB-47Hs and RB-47Ks being supported by half a dozen Martin RB-57s and about two dozen Lockheed U-2s. Tanker assets topped 1,000 for the first time, KC-97s outnumbering the KC-135A by more than two to one with respective totals of 745 and 322, while strategic airlift support was furnished by a fleet of 50 Douglas C-124 Globemasters. Finally, 59 North American F-86D Sabres equipped two Spanish-based fighter interceptor squadrons, these having been a fairly recent acquisition and one that was not destined to remain under SAC control for long.

Perhaps the most remarkable feature of the SAC line-up was the extent of its dependence upon Boeing as a prime source of equipment – indeed, it was not so much a case of dependence as domination, for just under 96 per cent of the entire complement traced its origins back to the drawing boards at Seattle, even though several hundred of the B-47s had actually

been produced by Douglas and Lockheed. For the next few years, Boeing was destined to retain its stranglehold as the major supplier of aircraft to SAC, largely by virtue of the fact that several hundred B-52s and KC-135s had still to be delivered, and about the only major inroad made into Boeing's well-entrenched position during the latter half of the 1950s was achieved by Convair, whose B-58A Hustler was ordered into quantity production for service with SAC. Even then, the Seattle-based company would undoubtedly have been more than reassured by its success with the Minuteman ICBM, it having been selected as prime contractor for this new weapon system in October 1958.

HOUND DOG

The overall capability of the manned bomber force was greatly enhanced by the arrival of the penultimate variant of the Stratofortress, the first B-52G being formally handed over to the 5th Bomb Wing at Travis AFB, California, less than 24 hours after the last B-36J was transferred to a well-earned retirement. Updating the Stratofortress avionics and fire control systems was matched by structural changes which offered significant range and payload benefits, while the G model was also the first to be designed from the outset as a missile platform, intended to carry 'side arms' in the shape of a brace of North American GAM-77 (later redesignated AGM-28) Hound Dogs. The fundamental objectives of Hound Dog were twofold in that it would

Far left, top: With Soviet defences growing ever more capable, it became necessary for bombers to descend in order to penetrate: this B-52G of the 68th BW is seen 'getting down to it', late 1970s. (Boeing)

Far left, centre: The year 1959 witnessed the demise of the Convair B-36 as a delivery system, the Biggs-based 95th BW disposing of its last aircraft on 12 February. Most of the once-proud fleet was subjected to the indignity of scrapping, but a few examples – such as this B-36J with the SAC Museum at Offutt – did escape to recall the days when the 'aluminium overcast' reigned supreme. (APN)

Far left, bottom: SAC acquired control of a couple of F-86D Sabre interceptor squadrons in 1958, the 431st FIS at Zaragoza and the 497th FIS at Torrejon. Apart from a few Convair TF-102As involved in the Hustler training programme in the early 1960s, these were the last fighters to serve with SAC. (North American)

Left: Ordered into quantity production in the late 1950s, Convair's delta-winged B-58 Hustler was the only type to present a serious challenge to Boeing's predominance as a supplier of bomber aircraft to Strategic Air Command. (APN)

permit heavily defended targets to be attacked without the need to expose the parent B-52 to unnecessary risk, while it would also aid penetrating bombers by enabling elements of an enemy's defensive network to be attacked and destroyed in advance of the passage of the B-52. Essentially an early application of the cruise missile principle, Hound Dog relied on a single Pratt and Whitney J52-P-3 turbojet engine for propulsion, a valuable bonus offered by this pylon-mounted weapon being that the engine could be used to augment the B-52's own battery of power-plants for 'heavyweight' take-offs; once airborne, the J52 could then be shut down and the Hound Dog's own fuel tanks topped up by the parent aircraft. The missile employed an integral inertial navigation system, and it could deliver a single W28 warhead with a yield of about 1Mt over a maximum range of around 500 nautical miles at high altitude

and high speed, or about 200 miles at low altitude and subsonic speed.

Ordered into production in October 1958, the first weapon was accepted by SAC's Commander-in-Chief, General Power, on 21 December 1959 and delivered to the 4135th SW at Eglin just two days later, this unit having been selected to assist the Air Research and Development Command with Category III operational testing. Early trials demonstrated a high standard of reli-

ability. The first launch by a SAC crew took place at the end of February 1960, while an even more impressive demonstration of capability occurred in April when a 4135th SW B-52G flew nearly 11,000 miles in the course of a 20-hour mission to the North Pole and back. Appropriately code-named Operation 'Blue Nose', this long sortie culminated in the launch of a missile which by all accounts worked satisfactorily despite having been subjected to a prolonged 'cold soak'. Programme planning anticipated the deployment of Hound Dog with some 29 B-52 squadrons, an objective which was accomplished during FY63 when the six B-52H squadrons all became operational. Other variants known to have been compatible with this weapon were the B-52E, B-52F and B-52G, Hound Dog being employed in conjunction with conventional gravity nuclear bombs housed in the B-52's internal weapons bay. The operational service of this weapon lasted just over fifteen years, the last examples eventually being retired in 1976.

QUAIL

Another air-launched missile to make its début at around this time was the GAM-72 (later ADM-20) Quail, but the development of this weapon was rather more protracted. Work on the programme was initiated in October 1952, and in February 1956 the McDonnell Aircraft Company was selected as the prime contractor, but further delays followed and a production contract was not let until the last day of December 1958. Powered by a single General Electric J85 turbojet engine, Quail was also intended to aid penetrating bombers to reach their designated targets, although it employed rather different techniques from those evident in Hound Dog in achieving this objective. Whereas the North American missile was essentially a weapon of destruction, Quail was intended to serve as a decoy by misleading enemy defences as to the precise whereabouts of the bombers they were seeking to destroy.

Despite its small size, Quail was packed with a variety of radar reflectors, electronic repeaters, chaff and infra-red simulators which between them produced a radar and IR image more or less identical to the signature of the far larger B-52; further confusion was likely to arise from the fact

Far left: With a Hound Dog missile nestling snugly beneath the starboard wing, an alert-dedicated B-52H awaits its crew at the start of an exercise. North American's Hound Dog entered service with the Eglin-based 4135th Strategic Wing at the end of 1959 and was eventually procured in substantial numbers, being one of the key B-52 weapons systems until the last examples were retired in 1976. Two of the missiles could be carried by each B-52. (USAF)

that it could be programmed to make at least two course changes and one variation in speed during its active life. Thus enemy defences were unlikely to be able to establish with any degree of certainty whether the target they were tracking was genuine. Unique in being the only decoy missile ever deployed by the US Air Force, Quail also offered security of numbers, it being possible for each suitably configured Stratofortress to carry a maximum of four of these devices internally in addition to gravity nuclear weapons. Range varied according to speed and altitude, but generally a Quail flying at Mach 0.85 and at 50,000ft could cover about 460 nautical miles, although

low-level operations reduced the range to as little as 39 miles. Operational planning anticipated the release of these decoys as the bomber force approached enemy territory, the hope being that they would saturate the defences and permit a high percentage of the bomber force to penetrate to its targets.

The first unit to acquire Quail was the Eglin-based 4135th SW, a number of pre-production examples being assigned to this unit from late February 1960 in order to participate in Category III operational testing. With most objectives achieved, delivery of production specimens began in September 1960, the 4135th SW again being the first recipient. Eventually, a total of fourteen squadrons received Quail, full-scale service introduction being accomplished between February 1961 – when the 4135th SW was deemed to be operationally ready with the new missile – and mid-April 1962. Like Hound Dog, the decoy missile was eventually retired in the latter half of the 1970s, the last examples leaving the inventory in 1978.

The first year of the new decade was significant in other ways, not least of which was the creation of the Joint Strategic Target Planning Staff during the summer. Situated alongside SAC Headquarters at Offutt AFB, the JSTPS came into existence at a time when the nuclear capability of the United States was being greatly diversified. Bomber aircraft were being joined by an increasing number of ICBMs, while the Navy's Polaris-

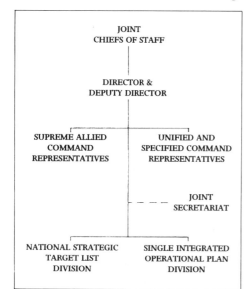

```
              JOINT
         CHIEFS OF STAFF
                |
            DIRECTOR &
         DEPUTY DIRECTOR
                |
   ┌────────────┴────────────┐
SUPREME ALLIED         UNIFIED AND
  COMMAND           SPECIFIED COMMAND
REPRESENTATIVES      REPRESENTATIVES
                │
                ┊           JOINT
                ┊        SECRETARIAT
                │
   ┌────────────┴────────────┐
NATIONAL STRATEGIC   SINGLE INTEGRATED
 TARGET LIST         OPERATIONAL PLAN
  DIVISION               DIVISION
```

Left: The relationship between those elements involved in preparing the Single Integrated Operational Plan and the associated National Strategic Target List is clearly evident in this 'wiring diagram' which covers Joint Strategic Target Planning Staff organization.

armed strategic submarine fleet would henceforth represent a very powerful force in its own right. Further, the deployment of tactical nuclear weapons with elements of the USAF at overseas bases also added greatly to the equation. With nuclear capabilities proliferating at a remarkable rate, it was clear that target planning needed to be brought under the overall control of a single authority if the various resources were to be employed effectively. It was this requirement which prompted the creation of the JSTPS, which had as its main brief the twin tasks of preparing a National Strategic Target List (NSTL) and a Single Integrated Operational Plan (SIOP), the latter being essentially a 'game plan' for nuclear war in which specific weapons systems were assigned to specific targets. In this way, it was hoped to obtain the best value from the resources available. Since SAC had acquired considerable expertise in strategic planning over the past few years, it was eminently sensible to locate the new body at Offutt, SAC's Commander-in-Chief being appointed to serve as the Director of the JSTPS which was made up of staff drawn from those elements of the US armed forces that were responsible for nuclear weapons delivery systems.

THE B-58 HUSTLER

On 1 August 1960, little more than two weeks before the JSTPS came into existence, SAC formally accepted the first operational examples of just such a system at Carswell AFB, Texas. This was the Convair B-58A Hustler, an elegant-looking and surprisingly large delta-winged aircraft which possessed quite remarkable performance characteristics – as it was soon to show in spectacular fashion. As a strategic bomber, however, the Hustler was something of a disappointment. It was always 'short-legged', unrefuelled range limitations being a particularly serious failing, whilst its high unit cost resulted in the procurement of just enough aircraft to equip two wings. Cost considerations continued to plague the Hustler throughout a service career which lasted less than ten years. Maintenance-intensive it certainly was, demanding extremely skilled technicians, and the cramped confines of the cockpit imposed strict limitations on the height and weight of those aircrew fortunate enough to be selected for service with the two bomb wings that operated this type, especially after the encapsulated ejection seats were introduced in 1962–63. If it failed to live up to expectations as a strategic bomber, as a record-breaker the Hustler had few peers, aircraft from the 43rd BW and the 305th BW repeatedly catching the headlines during 1961–63 with a succession of high-performance flights. The culmination of this phase of the Hustler's career came in October 1963, when the 305th BW's appropriately named 'Greased Lightning' hurtled 8,028 miles from Tokyo to London in just over eight and a half hours, bringing the number of official records claimed by the B-58 to nineteen. Unofficial records were also set on numerous occasions dur-

Below: Popularly known by SAC personnel as 'the Cadillac', the B-52H was the final version of Boeing's Stratofortress to enter service, a total of 102 aircraft being delivered between May 1961 and October 1962. It was also the only model to be powered by turbofan engines, its Pratt & Whitney TF33-P-3s being instrumental in giving this variant the greatest unrefuelled range of any member of the Stratofortress family. Seen at RAF Fairford in March 1964, the 72nd example of the B-52H to be completed carries the badge of the Homestead-based 19th Bomb Wing on the nose section below the cockpit. (APN)

ing the course of routine deployments, but these failed to gain the recognition which they perhaps deserved.

SAC had understandably been intimately involved in the Hustler's development programme for a number of years, providing personnel for the ARDC's 6592nd Test Squadron at Edwards AFB and organizing its own test unit, the 3958th Operational Test and Evaluation Squadron, at Carswell in March 1958, the latter unit doing much to smooth the path of service introduction and eventually being elevated to group status. The delivery of aircraft to the first true operational unit, the 43rd BW at Carswell, began in mid-March 1960, formal introduction following on 1 August coincident with SAC's assuming management responsibility for the entire B-58 programme. On that date SAC's commander, General Power, travelled to Carswell to accept the first full production example, one of a dozen Hustlers which were handed over to the 43rd BW on that date, most having previously been employed on test duties. Subsequently, during the summer of 1964, the 43rd moved to new quarters at Little Rock AFB, Arkansas, where it remained until deactivated at the end of January 1970. The second and last wing to obtain Hustlers was the 305th BW at Bunker Hill AFB, Indiana (later renamed Grissom AFB), which collected its first aircraft on 11 May 1961. Re-equipment was a fairly lengthy process and it was not until September of the following year that it resumed 'alert' duty, a matter of weeks before Hustler production ceased with the delivery of the 116th example on 26 October 1962.

On the same day as the final Hustlers were accepted by SAC, so too was the last Stratofortress delivered, the aircraft concerned being a B-52H which was assigned to the 4136th Strategic Wing at Minot AFB, North Dakota. Now, for the first time in its existence, SAC faced a future in which no new bomber aircraft were being produced or developed; indeed, the first half of the decade was very much a period of decline as far as manned bomber resources were concerned. Hardest hit was the B-47 fleet, which was reduced from more than 1,350 aircraft at the beginning of 1960 to just under 400 within the space of five years. With bomber production ceasing in the autumn of 1962, these losses were never

made good, but SAC's deterrent capability did, nevertheless, improve, largely by virtue of the rapid increase in the number of ICBMs assigned to 'alert' duty during the same period.

While it effectively marked the beginning of the end for the B-47 community, 1960 was memorable in other, more positive ways, most of which were aimed at enhancing the responsiveness of the Command. To begin with, SAC's objective of maintaining one-third of its bombers and tankers on ground alert was finally attained in May. Hard on the heels of that success came news of further efforts directed at increasing its retaliatory capability. A variation on the theme of dispersal, this involved the B-47 force and initially took the form of a test programme whereby selected units despatched small groups of aircraft and personnel to civilian airfields and other bases not under the authority of SAC. Test results soon revealed that this concept of dispersal was valid, and it was implemented during the Cuban missile crisis of late 1962 when the possibility of nuclear conflict seemed very real.

IMPROVED COMMAND AND CONTROL

By themselves, of course, bomber and missile assets would achieve little in the absence of adequate command and control facilities, so SAC also directed its energies towards improving communications links during the course of 1960. One important manifestation of this, which came into use in March, was 'Short Order', an HF-SSB (High-Frequency Single Side-Band) radio link which formed an integral part of the 'positive control' doctrine under which SAC bomber aircraft would not proceed beyond their fail-safe points in the absence of firm and authenticated orders. Airborne command posts also made their début in 1960, experience gained with the B-52 providing clear evidence that such a concept could be expanded to bolster command and control facilities, especially in the event of ground-based command posts being knocked out. Once again, extensive testing, conducted by a handful of suitably configured KC-135As of the Offutt-based 34th ARS during the last six months of 1960, confirmed the validity of the concept, each specially modified aircraft being packed with sophisticated

communications gear and normally manned by a battle staff led by an SAC general officer. Subsequently conducted under the code-name 'Looking Glass', airborne command post operations were initiated on a permanent, round-the-clock basis on 3 February 1961, and at least one fully manned Boeing EC-135 or E-4 has been kept aloft ever since. The system was considerably expanded in later years, when it became known as the Post-Attack Command and Control System (PACCS).

The year 1961 was in many ways one of mixed fortunes for SAC. A real body-blow was struck in March when, in his defence budget speech, President John F. Kennedy revealed that plans to procure the North American B-70 Valkyrie would be abandoned in order to permit scarce financial resources to be redirected elsewhere. This announcement did not quite spell the end for the XB-70 since it was decided to complete three aircraft to serve as test-beds for researching flight at speeds of around Mach 3. However, the XB-70 project proved to be dogged by misfortune, since the third example was ultimately shelved and one of the two which did fly was destroyed in a collision with an F-104 chase aircraft. In the same speech Kennedy also directed SAC to move to a heightened state of readiness, stipulating that the Command should endeavour to increase ground alert forces to no less than 50 per cent, although the extra personnel required would be drawn from resources taken from a number of B-47 wings earmarked for deactivation as phasing out was accelerated. The withdrawal of

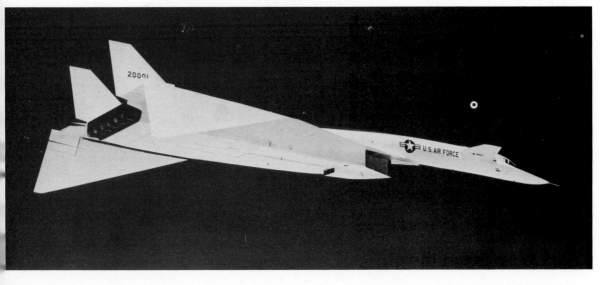

the Stratojet had begun as early as 1957, but most of the early candidates for 'the bone-yard' were RB-47Es, pure bomber aircraft being virtually unaffected until 1960. In that year three wings disposed of this type, the 43rd, 44th, and 320th BWs, and these were followed into limbo by six more units in 1961, the 19th, 305th, 308th, 321st, 341st and 379th BWs. Plans to deactivate six more wings and a similar number of KC-97 tanker squadrons were held up temporarily in the light of the Berlin crisis of 1961, and the following year witnessed only the departure of the 70th BW.

However, Kennedy's statement also included a request for additional funding for the Skybolt air-launched ballistic missile (ALBM), and this was duly agreed to by Congress. Closely allied to Skybolt was the B-52H, this turbofan-powered variant of the Stratofortress being designated as the launch platform. The first example of the new aircraft to reach SAC joined the 379th BW at Wurtsmith AFB, Michigan, on 9 May 1961. The Command eventually acquired 102 copies of 'the Cadillac', but these had to make do with Hound Dog, for Skybolt fell foul of cancellation just before the end of 1962, the decision to terminate this pro-gramme being justified on the grounds of high cost and questionable operational value.

THE CUBAN MISSILE CRISIS

Somewhat ironically, Skybolt's cancellation came hot on the heels of the Cuban missile crisis, an event which provided SAC with the opportunity to assess its preparedness for full-scale nuclear conflict and one which must have caused the incumbent President to reflect on the 'Bay of Pigs' adventure which had cast such a cloud over the early days of his term of office. On this occasion, however, Kennedy came out of the affair with his reputation much enhanced. Indica-tions of a Soviet build-up on the island of Cuba prompted increased surveillance flights by U-2s, and it was one of these aircraft which brought back incontrover-

Above: The turbofan-powered B-52H was easily the most cap-able variant of the Stratofortress but its overall effectiveness was to some extent compromised by the December 1962 decision to cancel the Skybolt ALBM; the 102 B-52Hs eventually had to settle for the AGM-28 Hound Dog. (USAF)

Right: In view of its position as the man-ager of the deterrent force, it was hardly surprising that SAC moved to a much heightened alert state during the Cuban Missile Crisis of 1962. Airborne alert activity by the B-52 was stepped up, while B-47s at home and over-seas were brought to full combat readiness. (APN)

TABLE 9: B-52 VARIANTS, JANUARY 1963	
Variant	**Wing**
B-52B	95 BW
B-52C	99 BW
B-52D	28 BW, 92 SAW, 4047 SW, 4128 SW, 4130 SW, 4138 SW, 4141 SW, 4170 SW, 4245 SW
B-52E	6 SAW, 11 SAW, 4043 SW, 4123 SW
B-52F	7 BW, 4134 SW, 4228 SW, 4238 SW
B-52G	5 BW, 42 BW, 72 BW, 97 BW, 4038 SW, 4039 SW, 4126 SW, 4135 SW, 4137 SW, 4241 SW
B-52H	19 BW, 379 BW, 4042 SW, 4133 SW, 4136 SW, 4239 SW

Note: The 93rd BW was operating both B-52B and B-52F models in 1963.

ible evidence of Soviet intentions on 14 October. Further U-2 sorties over the next few days brought further evidence, but it was not until 22 October that Kennedy broke the news of the impending crisis when he announced an immediate blockade of Cuba and demanded the removal of those missiles that were already in place.

Against this background of rising tension, SAC implemented a number of measures aimed at increasing its already impressive retaliatory capability. Battle staffs convened, personnel were hastily recalled, ground alert was stepped up, B-47s departed to dispersal bases, airborne alert forces took to the sky and every available ICBM was prepared for flight. Meanwhile the rest of the world held its breath and waited for the first signs of a break in the crisis. It was not long in coming. Negotiations behind the scenes resulted in the Soviet Union agreeing on 28 October to remove the missiles, a *quid pro quo* being that the Jupiter IRBMs located in Italy and Turkey would also be phased out; an announcement to this effect was made by Kennedy on 24 January 1963.

By that time matters were back to normal. The immediate threat of war had been averted and SAC had quietly dropped back to routine levels of alert while pressing ahead with plans to resume the process of disposing of both the B-47 and KC-97. As part of this programme, six more B-47 wings – the 2nd, 22nd, 68th, 96th, 306th and 340th – all stood down in 1963, as did seven KC-97 tanker squadrons. These reductions inevitably had some impact on 'Reflex Action', and B-47s ceased 'alert' duties at Ben Guerir, Nouasseur and Sidi Slimane

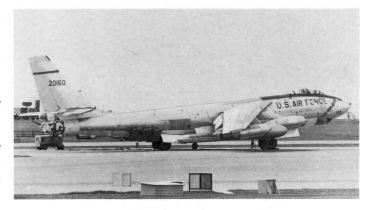

during 1963. The operation was henceforth centred on three Spanish bases, four British bases and Elmendorf in Alaska, while the generally similar 'Air Mail' activity continued at Andersen. Overseas-based tanker task forces were also cut, KC-97 elements at Kindley AFB, Bermuda, and at the Canadian bases at Churchill, Cold Lake and Frobisher all ceasing operations in 1963, although ground alert-dedicated KC-97s remained very much in evidence at Namao in Canada, at Goose Bay, Labrador, at Harmon AFB, Newfoundland, and at Sondrestrom, Greenland.

As 1964 dawned, SAC was still very much in a state of flux, but it was clearly determined to meet the challenge inherent in making the transition from the status of being a pure bomber force to one based on both missiles and aircraft. Other equally demanding challenges would have to be faced in the years ahead, not the least of which was the need to come to terms with the rigours of war: in common with other elements of the US armed forces, SAC was on the brink of combat in South-East Asia.

Above: All three of the Moroccan installations ceased supporting the B-47 in 1963, but 'Reflex Action' did continue elsewhere for two more years, Upper Heyford in England being one of the last bases to host Stratojets engaged in this mission. This particular B-47E, from the 509th BW at Plattsburgh, is seen at Upper Heyford and is unusual in that it carries the 'Tee Town' ECM pod on the fuselage side. (APN)

Mors ab Alto*

FROM PEACE TO WAR

For Strategic Air Command, the third decade of its existence was perhaps the most difficult yet. Having evolved into what was undeniably the most powerful bomber force the world had ever seen, it was, as 1964 opened, fast losing what could be called 'the personal touch': no longer would the bomber be viewed as the principal means of deterrence, nor would SAC be perceived as the sole instrument of that policy. This is not to say that the bomber was finished – subsequent events were to prove that that was far from true – but rather that it would in future form only one element of what eventually became known as the 'strategic triad', submarine-launched ballistic missiles and land-based ICBMs providing the other two components.

Reductions in the size of the B-47 fleet continued throughout 1964, four more units – the 40th, 301st, 303rd and 384th BWs – all disposing of their aircraft, as did some five KC-97 tanker squadrons. Thus, by the end of the year, only eight pure bomber wings still used the Stratojet, the once-proud fleet having dwindled in size to less than 450 aircraft. For the first time, the B-52 occupied a position of numerical supremacy with some 600 or so examples on hand, force strength being completed by just under 100 B-58A Hustlers. In-flight refuelling resources at the end of the year comprised no fewer than 679 Stratotankers and about 190 KC-97s. Most of the former were KC-135As, but there was also a modest number of EC-135s which constituted the principal element of the expanding Post Attack Command Control System. Reconnaissance assets had also been in decline: fewer than 30 RB-47 'ferrets' remained active with the 55th SRW, while an even smaller number of U-2s served with the 4080th SRW on more conventional, high-altitude photographic tasks. In distinct contrast, missile forces continued to expand as more and more Minutemen entered the inventory, and 1964 was noteworthy for the fact that alert-assigned ICBMs finally gained parity with the number of alert bombers on 21 April, thereafter becoming the predominant element in the deterrent capability.

Continuing reductions in bomber strength in turn had a marked effect on the composition of overseas-based 'Reflex' echelons. The spring of 1964 witnessed the closure of Fairford and Greenham Common in England as well as Zaragoza in Spain; at the same time, the 'Air Mail' ground alert force at Andersen acquired greater effectiveness when it traded B-47s for B-52s although, as will be seen, nuclear alert very soon became a less important feature of day-to-day activity. Tanker forces also declined, Sondrestrom in Greenland and Namao in Canada shutting down as KC-97 bases in June; on the other hand, more modern equipment reached Goose Bay, Labrador, in October when the KC-97 was supplanted by the KC-135. Thus by the end of 1964 'Reflex' bombers continued to operate from just five bases, Brize Norton and Upper Heyford in Britain, Moron and Torrejon in Spain and Elmendorf in Alaska. Finally, only Harmon AFB in Newfoundland still hosted Boeing's portly KC-97.

VIETNAM

By this time developments on the other side of the world had led to SAC's returning to a combat role for the first time in more than a decade. Once again, South-East Asia was the area of operations and Vietnam proved to be the catalyst for a ten-year effort which also witnessed the devastation of large areas of Cambodia and Laos. Although it was perhaps the most spectacular and visible manifestation of SAC activity in South-East Asia, the Command's involvement in this long conflict was by no means confined to bombing, for tanker and reconnaissance units were also heavily committed throughout the main period of US support between 1964 and 1973; indeed, it was the latter role which provided SAC with its first taste of

"Death from Above' – motto of the 17th Bomb Wing

warfare at this time, predating the massive escalation which took place after the celebrated Tonkin Gulf incident of August 1964.

SAC was, of course, no stranger to the area. RB-47Hs of the 55th SRW had been regular visitors in the course of routine intelligence-gathering flights, but efforts to acquire information about North Vietnamese intentions, actions and capabilities were stepped up at the beginning of 1964, and one of the first intimations of increasing US interest was the hurried deployment of some 4080th SRW U-2s from Davis-Monthan to Bien Hoa in South Vietnam. Initially given the code name 'Lucky Dragon', and later using a succession of titles including 'Trojan Horse', 'Giant Dragon' and 'Olympic Torch', these operations first received Presidential authorization at the end of 1963. The primary objective of the Lockheed aircraft was to obtain information on the enemy's infiltration network, and the U-2 was quickly in action, one or two sorties being flown daily over the borders with Laos, Cambodia and North Vietnam with effect from early 1964. As the US commitment increased – and before the threat from surface-to-air missiles (SAMs) prevented further incursions – U-2 activity expanded to include overflights of North Vietnam, and data gained on potential targets during these sorties was later put to good use in the prolonged 'Rolling Thunder' bombing and interdiction campaign of 1965–68. The 'Dragon Lady' also brought back the first positive proof of

North Vietnamese efforts to increase the country's defensive capability when, on 5 April 1965, one of the Bien Hoa-based U-2s photographed the first of many SAM sites.

At the same time as U-2 photographic reconnaissance was beginning to yield valuable information, so too were efforts aimed at obtaining data on North Vietnam's 'electronic order of battle' being expanded. RB-47Hs and the much less numerous ERB-47H were initially used to obtain this material, the so-called 'Box Top' missions being staged out of Yokota, Japan, under the management of the 3rd Air Division's Detachment One. At the beginning, 'Box Top' formed only a small part of the 55th SRW's global activity, but these peripheral missions over the Tonkin Gulf heralded the start of an intelligence-gathering effort which, at its height, involved several aircraft and 24-hour coverage of the war zone. SAC's principal 'ferret' platform for the best part of a decade, the RB-47H bore the brunt of the elint/sigint (electronic intelligence/ signals intelligence) workload until about 1966, when the RC-135 began to assume greater responsibility for this valuable mission. Eventually, the latter type took over completely, and continuing efforts to improve the Command's capability resulted in a bewildering proliferation of RC-135 sub-types, several of which were employed in the combat zone. Insofar as any aspect of strategic reconnaissance may be described as 'visible', these two operations were fairly obvious right from the start in that they

Below: As the B-47 fleet was winding down, so too was the KC-97 disappearing from the scene, tanker task forces at a number of overseas bases terminating operations in 1963–64. Indeed, by the end of 1964, the 'Strat' was fast becoming a rare sight, only Harmon AFB in Newfoundland still hosting the type. (APN)

relied on manned aircraft which possessed certain distinctive characteristics. The glider-like appearance of the long-winged U-2, for example, rendered it 'visible' in a way which was probably only surpassed by the RB-47, a type that could never be relied upon to keep a low profile – as anyone who has ever witnessed a Stratojet departure will know only too well!

'LIGHTNING BUG'

The third element of SAC's reconnaissance 'triad' to undertake combat operations in Vietnam was, however, truly 'black' – the long-running RPV (remotely piloted vehicle) or drone operation. It is fair to say that very little of the small amount of information which has filtered out concerning this fascinating subject has originated from SAC. As with the U-2, the management of drone activity was entrusted to the 4080th SRW at Davis-Monthan, this endeavour being declared operational on 1 July 1963 when it, in essence, formed part of the 4028th SRS. It was known then simply as the 'Lightning Bug' group, but the fast expanding level of drone activity necessitated the bestowal of squadron status in July 1965, when it was designated the 4025th SRS. By this time, of course, RPVs had been flying combat missions for just under a year, deployment to the war zone having taken place within days of the Tonkin Gulf incident.

Orders to move to the Far East had come within a matter of hours. The base chosen to host the new units was Kadena, Okinawa, which was given the designation Operational Location Eight (OL-8), and two Lockheed DC-130A Hercules 'mother ships', numerous Ryan 147B 'Lightning Bug' drones and many USAF and contractor personnel were very quickly shipped out. The first mission, staged on 20 August, was less than successful in that the primary drone failed to launch at the desired moment, although fortunately a back-up RPV was available and this did work more or less as advertised. Perhaps more embarrassing was the fact that the original primary drone chose to part company with its DC-130A en route back to Kadena, the Ryan 147B performing a spectacular dive into the Pacific Ocean from an altitude of about 24,000ft. This was not an auspicious start, and the early part of the programme did not augur well, most of the first dozen or so missions being plagued by problems; further disruption arose from two typhoon alerts which necessitated a hasty withdrawal to Guam. Then, within a month of arriving at Kadena, the entire operation was transferred to Bien Hoa, but it remained here for just eight days as it fast became evident that the move was ill-conceived for a variety of reasons. Back at Kadena, the performance of the RPVs at last began to show signs of improvement, and by the time the second attempt to become established at Bien Hoa (OL-20) had taken place in early October the overall picture was much more satisfactory, two reasonably successful missions being accomplished by the 'Blue Springs' team within days of the move. By the end of the year 'Blue Springs' had completed twenty missions, accumulated some valuable intelligence, and laid a solid base for future operations from Bien Hoa.

TANKER OPERATIONS

The summer of 1964 also witnessed the start of another long-running endeavour in support of the war, and this was, on occasions, to tax SAC to the limit. At that time, of course, aerial refuelling capability was more than adequate to meet projected needs, SAC's still-expanding fleet of KC-135s being backed up by a dwindling number of KC-97s; in addition, Pacific Air Forces, United States Air Forces in Europe and Tactical Air Command all numbered some examples of the KB-50J among their resources, these generally being relied upon

Above: The third major SAC reconnaissance tool employed in Vietnam was the 'Lightning Bug'. Launching the Ryan 147 pilotless drones was effected from mother ships like the DC-130A Hercules seen here complete with a drone at Davis-Monthan AFB, Arizona, in November 1969. (Author)

Left: Trailing its pod-mounted refuelling drogues, a Boeing KB-50J of the Sculthorpe-based 420th ARS simulates a 'hook-up' with an F-100D Super Sabre and an F-101C Voodoo at a British air display in the early 1960s. (MAP)

to satisfy immediate tactical needs. That was certainly true in South-East Asia, where PACAF KB-50Js stationed at Yokota and Kadena had been deploying in small numbers to such bases as Takhli and Tan Son Nhut to furnish aerial refuelling support to tactical aircraft engaged in combat duty. However, the loss of one of these elderly aircraft on take-off from Takhli in October prompted a detailed inspection of the remaining airframes, and this, in turn, resulted in a permanent grounding order when severe corrosion was detected. SAC had been planning to establish a KC-135 tanker task force at Kadena during the course of 1965, and the unanticipated non-availability of the KB-50J necessitated urgent action to overcome the shortfall. Planning initiatives for the Kadena force were conducted under the code-name 'Tamale Pete', and the activation of the 4252nd Strategic Wing took place on 12 January 1965, followed by the first operational mission on 25 January.

As a matter of fact, this was not the first time that SAC tankers had provided support to PACAF fighter aircraft engaged in combat operations. Several months earlier, on 9 June 1964, four KC-135s had rendezvoused with eight F-100 Super Sabres near Da Nang, dispensing fuel to the fighters which were on their way to attack anti-aircraft artillery emplacements on the Plain of Jars in northern Laos. Following the post-strike refuelling of a couple of F-100s, the KC-135s returned to Clark Air Base in the Philippines. Known as the 'Yankee Team' Tanker Task Force, the Clark-based element had been created on 7 June when four KC-135s at Hickam and two at Andersen had been directed to move to the Philippines in response to an order from the Joint Chiefs of Staff (JCS). It had been intended to stage another mission on 13 June, but this was abandoned and the JCS duly authorized the release of the 'Yankee Team' aircraft, which quickly departed from Clark.

Below: A quartet of bomb-laden Republic F-105D Thunderchiefs formates with a SAC KC-135A Stratotanker *en route* to a strike in North Vietnam. SAC's refuelling support of the war in South-East Asia began in June 1964 and was instrumental in enabling tactical elements of the Pacific Air Forces to carry the war deep into the heartland of the north. (USAF)

The KC-135 was back on 5 August, and 'Yankee Team' resumed operations from Clark with eight aircraft in the wake of the Tonkin Gulf incident. This effectively marked the start of SAC's aerial refuelling support of the Vietnam War, and 29 'hook-ups' were accomplished during the first eight days of operations. Initially involving rotational aircraft and crews, the task force changed its name to 'Foreign Legion' at the beginning of September, and soon afterwards it was revealed that it would relinquish its commitment to the forthcoming Kadena-based force. This was given the nickname 'Young Tiger', nomenclature which ultimately became all-embracing in that it covered tanker operations in South-East Asia right up to late December 1975 when the last KC-135s departed from U-Tapao in Thailand.

Even as Kadena was welcoming additional Stratotankers, the size of the 'Foreign Legion' force was slightly reduced, falling from eight to six aircraft by 1 March 1965. On that date 'Foreign Legion' ceased operations at Clark; four of the KC-135s immediately moved on to Don Muang in Thailand, where they formed the newly created 'Tiger Cub' Tanker Task Force, while the other two joined the 4252nd SW operation at Kadena.

B-52 AT WAR

Perhaps of greater significance, in that it signalled SAC's willingness to employ the massive Stratofortress in a conventional bombing role, was the decision to increase the number of B-52s stationed at Andersen AFB, Guam. Preparations effectively got under way in mid-February when the 7th and 320th BWs despatched a total of 30 B-52Fs, a similar number of accompanying KC-135s making their way to Kadena. By mid-year, the latter base hosted some 45 aircraft of this type, one-third of them allocated to 'Young Tiger' tactical operations and the remainder constituting the 'Arc Light' tanker force. As it turned out, the first 'Arc Light' mission did not take place for several months, resistance to employing the B-52 in a tactical capacity arising partly from political considerations and partly from doubt as to its value in such operations. Eventually, though, ComUSMACV (Commander US Military Assistance Command Vietnam) General William C. West-

moreland managed to obtain clearance to commit 'the big stick' to action, and the first strike was staged on 18 June when 27 B-52Fs

TABLE 10: SAC ORDER OF BATTLE, DECEMBER 1964				
Division	Base	Unit	Components	Equipment
2nd Air Force (Barksdale AFB, La)				
4th SAD	Grand Forks, ND	319th BW	46 BS	B-52H
			905 ARS	KC-135A
	Grand Forks, ND	321st SMW	No squadrons assigned	LGM-30F due
	K. I. Sawyer, Mi	410th BW	644 BS	B-52H
			46 ARS	KC-135A
19th AD	Barksdale, La	2nd BW	20 BS	B-52F
			913 ARS	KC-135A
	Carswell, Tx	7th BW	9 BS	B-52F
			7 ARS	KC-135A
	Bergstrom, Tx	340th BW	486 BS	B-52D
			910 ARS	KC-135A
40th AD	Wurtsmith, Mi	379th BW	524 BS	B-52H
			920 ARS	KC-135A
	Kincheloe, Mi	449th BW	716 BS	B-52H
			908 ARS	KC-135A
	Selfridge, Mi	500th ARW	44/307 ARS	KC-97G (44 ARS deact. 15/12/64)
42nd AD	Blytheville, Ar	97th BW	340 BS	B-52G
			97 ARS	KC-135A
	Columbus, Miss	454th BW	736 BS	B-52F
			901 ARS	KC-135A
810th SAD	Forbes, Ks	55th SRW	38/343 SRS	EB-47E(TT), ERB/ RB-47H
			548 SMS	CGM-16E Atlas E
	Minot, ND	450th BW	720 BS	B-52H
			906 ARS	KC-135A
	Minot, ND	455th SMW	740/741/742 SMS	LGM-30B Minuteman I
816th SAD	Altus, Ok	11th SAW	26 BS	B-52E
			96 ARS	KC-135A
			577 SMS	HGM-16F Atlas F
	Clinton-Sherman, Ok	70th BW	6 BS	B-52E
			902 ARS	KC-135A
	Sheppard, Tx	494th BW	864 BS	B-52D
			900 ARS	KC-135A
818th SAD	Lincoln, Ne	98th SAW	343/344/345 BS	B-47E
			551 SMS	HGM-16F Atlas F
	Lincoln, NE	307th BW	370/371/372 BS	B-47E
			4362 PACCS	EB-47L (deact. 24/12/64)
	Offutt, Ne	385th SAW (deact. 15/12/64)	34 ARS	KC-135A
			549 SMS	CGM-16D Atlas D
825th SAD	Little Rock, Ar	43rd BW	63/64/65 BS	B-58A
			70 ARS	KC-135A
	Bunker Hill, In	305th BW	364/365/366 BS	B-58A
			68 ARS	KC-135A
	Little Rock, Ar	308th SMW	373/374 SMS	LGM-25C Titan II

Continued on p. 91

pulverized a suspected Viet Cong base in Binh Duong province with a mixture of 750lb and 1,000lb 'iron' bombs.

Needless to say, this raid generated considerable controversy, further argument being brought about by the fact that two of the force of 30 aircraft collided during the course of pre-strike refuelling with the loss of eight personnel, while another B-52F had to abandon the mission after failing to take on fuel; even more damagingly, a post-strike examination of the target area by Special Forces personnel revealed little evidence of significant damage. Westmoreland, however, was undaunted by such controversy, arguing successfully for the continued use of the B-52, and by the end of 1965 at least 100 more 'Arc Light' missions had taken place, happily without loss. Although most of the missions were targeted against Viet Cong base areas, some direct tactical support was also provided, most notably in November when elements of the Marine Corps and the Army's 1st Cavalry Division came under concentrated attack after stumbling across a major enemy base in the Ia Drang valley. Timely intervention by B-52s and other aircraft prevented a potential disaster, the 96 B-52 sorties that were flown over the next few days, resulting in the delivery of just under 1,800 tons of bombs.

At that time, the B-52F variant of the Stratofortress was the only one committed to combat and, while it clearly packed a powerful punch, it could carry at most just 51 bombs, 27 internally with 24 more on underwing racks. The next version to see combat was the B-52D, which joined the fray in the spring of 1966 when aircraft of the 28th and 484th BWs took over the responsibility for 'Arc Light' missions. These aircraft, in contrast, possessed real 'muscle', having been subjected to the so-called 'Big Belly' modification project in the months leading up to deployment. Alterations to the weapons bay permitted the B-52D to accommodate no fewer than 84 500lb or 750lb bombs internally; underwing racks raised the grand total to 108 bombs and the maximum payload was now of the order of 60,000lb, which meant that a single aircraft was able to lay down a veritable 'carpet' of bombs. When one recalls that the 'Arc Light' bombers usually operated in cells of three aircraft, one can

8th Air Force (Westover AFB, Ma)

6th AD	Wright-Patterson, Oh	17th BW	34 BS	B-52E
			922 ARS	KC-135A
	Dow, Me	397th BW	596 BS	B-52G
			71 ARS	KC-135A
	Griffiss, NY	416th BW	668 BS	B-52G
			41 ARS	KC-135A
13th SMD	F. E. Warren, Wy	90th SMW	319/320/321/400 SMS	LGM-30B Minuteman I
	F. E. Warren, Wy	389th SMW	565 SMS	CGM-16D Atlas D (deact. 1/12/64)
			566 SMS	CGM-16E Atlas E
	Lowry, Co	451st SMW	724/725 SMS	HGM-25A Titan I
17th SAD	Whiteman, Mo	351st SMW	508/509/510 SMS	LGM-30B Minuteman I
	McConnell, Ks	381st SMW	532/533 SMS	LGM-25C Titan II
45th AD	Loring, Me	42nd BW	69/70 BS	B-52G
			42 ARS	KC-135A
57th AD	Westover, Ma	99th BW	346/348 BS	B-52C
	Seymour-Johnson, NC	68th BW	51 BS	B-52G
			911 ARS	KC-135A
	Westover, Ma	499th ARW	99 ARS	KC-135A
			384 ARS	KC-97G
801st AD	Lockbourne, Oh	301st ARW	91/321 ARS	KC-135A
	Lockbourne, Oh	376th BW	512/513/514 BS	EB-47E
			4363 PACCS	EB-47L
817th AD	Pease, NH	100th BW	349/350/351 BS	B-47E
			100 ARS	KC-97G
	Pease, NH	509th BW	393/715/830 BS	B-47E
			509 ARS	KC-97G
820th SAD	Plattsburgh, NY	380th SAW	528/529/530 BS	B-47E
			4365 PACCS	EB-47L (deact. 24/12/64)
			380 ARS	KC-135A
			556 SMS	HGM-16F Atlas F
822nd AD	Eglin, Fl	39th BW	62 BS	B-52G
	Robins, Ga	465th BW	781 BS	B-52G
			912 ARS	KC-135A
	Turner, Ga	484th BW	824 BS	B-52D
			919 ARS	KC-135A
823rd AD	Homestead, Fl	19th BW	28 BS	B-52H
			407 ARS	KC-135A
	Ramey, Puerto Rico	72nd BW	60 BS	B-52G
			915 ARS	KC-135A
	McCoy, Fl	306th BW	367 BS	B-52D
			306 ARS	KC-135A
–	Dover AFB, De	11th ARS		KC-97G
–	Otis AFB, Ma	19th ARS		KC-97G
–	McGuire AFB, NJ	305th ARS		KC-97G
–	Harmon, Newfoundland	4081st SW	376 ARS	KC-97G (TDY elements)
–	Goose Bay, Labrador	4082nd SW		TDY elements
–	Thule, Greenland	4083rd ABW		TDY elements
–	Sondrestrom, Greenland	4084th ABG		TDY elements

Continued on p. 92

perhaps begin to appreciate the extent of the devastation that ensued, huge areas of Laos, Cambodia and South Vietnam being laid waste by these strikes in eight years of war.

During that time, exactly 124,532 of the scheduled 126,663 B-52 sorties had culminated in successful bomb release, the total amount of ordnance delivered surpassing 2.63 million tons. By itself, this figure may be hard to visualize but some perspective may be gained from the fact that it was handsomely in excess of the 2.15 million tons of munitions expended in Europe and the Far East during the whole of the Second World War. For the United States, the cost was 29 aircraft lost, seventeen as a direct result of enemy fire (all the aircraft, incidentally, falling victim to North Vietnam's fearsome defensive network) and twelve to other operational causes. Many B-52 crew members did survive, however, some being rescued and others joining the ever-growing list of prisoners-of-war.

PROJECT 'FAST FLY'

Although 1965 is perhaps best remembered as the year in which SAC's conventional activities in South-East Asia began to proliferate, this increase was accompanied by a reduction in its nuclear strike capability elsewhere in the world. After almost eight years of operation, 'Reflex Action' was finally terminated in Europe at the end of March, when 'alert' forces at Brize Norton, Upper Heyford, Moron and Torrejon stood down and the B-47s engaged in this duty were returned to US bases within a matter of days. This heralded the end of the line for the B-47, and it was followed in October by Project 'Fast Fly', the code name given to the accelerated phasing-out of the five remaining B-47 wings, the 9th, 98th, 100th, 380th and 509th. It had originally been intended to eliminate these units from the inventory by June 1966, but 'Fast Fly' changed all that: the 98th, 380th and 509th ceased 'alert' duty very quickly and had disposed of their remaining aircraft by the end of the year. The 9th SAW at Mountain Home and the 100th BW at Pease continued to stand alert until the very last day of 1965, both units then wasting little time in consigning their aircraft to storage. Subsequently, on 11 February, SAC's employment of the Stratojet as a pure bomber came to an

end when the last two B-47Es left Mountain Home and Pease *en route* to retirement. Some examples of the Stratojet did still fly, however, RB-47Hs of the 55th SRW soldiering on in the task of intelligence-gathering until 29 December 1967.

15th Air Force (March AFB, Ca)				
12th SAD	Biggs, Tx	95th BW	334 BS	B-52B
			917 ARS	KC-135A
	Davis-Monthan, Az	390th SMW	570/571 SMS	LGM-25C Titan II
	Davis-Monthan, Az	4080th SRW	4028 SRS	U-2, DC-130, 'Lightning Bug' drone
14th SAD	Travis, Ca	5th BW	23 BS	B-52G
			916 ARS	KC-135A
	Mather, Ca	320th BW	441 BS	B-52F
			904 ARS	KC-135A
	Beale, Ca	456th SAW	744 BS	B-52G
			903 ARS	KC-135A
			851 SMS	HGM-25A Titan I
18th SAD	Fairchild, Wa	92nd SAW	325 BS	B-52D
			92 ARS	KC-135A
			567 SMS	CGM-16E Atlas E
	Larson, Wa	462nd SAW	768 BS	B-52D
			43 ARS	KC-135A
			568 SMS	HGM-25A Titan I
22nd SAD	Walker, NM	6th SAW	24/40 BS	B-52E
			6 ARS	KC-135A
			579 SMS	HGM-16F Atlas F
	Schilling, Ks	310th SAW	379/380/381 BS	B-47E
			310 ARS	KC-135A
			550 SMS	HGM-16F Atlas F
47th SAD	March, Ca	22nd BW	2 BS	B-52B
			22 ARS	KC-135A
	Castle, Ca	93rd BW	328/329 BS	B-52F
			4017 CCTS	B-52F
			93/924 ARS	KC-135A
813th SAD	Mountain Home, Id	9th SAW	1/5/99 BS	B-47E
			4364 PACCS	EB-47L
			9 ARS	KC-97G
			569 SMS	HGM-25A Titan I
	Malmstrom, Mt	341st SMW	10/12/490 SMS	LGM-30A Minuteman I
819th SAD	Dyess, Tx	96th SAW	337 BS	B-52E
			578 SMS	HGM-16F Atlas F
	Amarillo, Tx	461st BW	764 BS	B-52D
			909 ARS	KC-135A
821st SAD	Ellsworth, SD	28th BW	77 BS	B-52D
			28 ARS	KC-135A
	Ellsworth, SD	44th SMW	66/67/68 SMS	LGM-30B Minuteman I
			850 SMS	HGM-25A Titan I
	Glasgow, Mt	91st BW	322 BS	B-52D
			907 ARS	KC-135A

'Fast Fly' was also extended to cover the few remaining KC-97 tanker squadrons, the 9th ARS at Mountain Home claiming the honour of being the last unit to stand alert with the KC-97 when it ended this commitment on 10 November 1965. The gradual retirement of the KC-97 continued until 21 December, the last two units to turn in their aircraft being the 100th ARS at Pease and the 384th ARS at Westover, and henceforth, with the exception of 'hack' aircraft like the C-47 and T-29, SAC controlled an all-jet force, dominated by the B-52 and KC-135.

Since all five B-47 wings involved in 'Fast Fly' were possessed of distinguished histories, SAC elected to retain these units, a decision which involved some realignment and a certain amount of redesignation. Two of the units, the 380th SAW and the 509th BW at Plattsburgh and Pease respectively, continued to serve as elements of the deterrent force, both acquiring B-52s during the course of 1966, but the other three all experienced great change in that they assumed responsibility for missions and resources far removed from those previ-

ously undertaken. Nowhere was this change more evident than with the 9th SAW, which shifted from Mountain Home to Beale on 25 June 1966, taking over assets previously assigned to the 4200th Strategic Wing and simultaneously being redesignated a Strategic Reconnaissance Wing. In future, it would operate the Lockheed SR-71, SAC's newest and most potent addition to the reconnaissance force. Capable of performance levels which are still unmatched, the SR-71 routinely operated at altitudes in excess of 80,000ft and at speeds of the order of Mach 3. It could survey 60,000 square miles in just one hour with a variety of sensor systems, including infrared, radar and optical devices.

At the time the 9th SRW took over from the 4200th SW, the 'Blackbird' was still far from being a fully operational system, the first example to reach SAC being a two-seat SR-71B which was delivered on 7 January 1966. That claim could not, however, be made of another Lockheed product, the U-2. The management of operations by this high flyer – and of the increasingly impor-

Top: The first examples of the Stratofortress to undertake combat action were B-52Fs drawn from the 7th and 320th Bomb Wings, the example depicted here being from the latter unit. As a temporary measure to minimize the risk of detection, these aircraft featured a hastily applied coat of black paint on their bellies. (APN)
Above: Photographed moments before making contact with a KC-135A, this B-52D is typical of those which bore the brunt of conventional bombing missions during the Vietnam War. (Boeing)

tant 'Lightning Bug' drone reconnaissance programme – was entrusted to the 100th SRW, which inherited the mantle of responsibility from the 4080th SRW at Davis-Monthan with effect from 25 June 1966. The remaining 'Fast Fly' unit, the 98th SAW at Lincoln, was perhaps less fortunate in that redesignation was not accompanied by new equipment. Instead, as the 98th Strategic Wing, it moved to Torrejon, Spain, where it replaced the 3970th SW on 25 June and subsequently managed in-flight refuelling resources detached to European bases for short periods of rotational duty.

AIR POWER BUILDS UP

In the Far East, the year 1966 was notable for a steady expansion in the effort directed towards supporting the war. As previously noted, the B-52D assumed responsibility for the 'Arc Light' mission during the spring, an event which was predated by the activation of the 4133rd Bomb Wing, Provisional, at Andersen. This immediately took over the task of managing rotational bomber forces assigned to this theatre, US-based wings usually spending about six months on Guam before being relieved. Increasing demand for tanker support also prompted the activation of another task force in Thailand, the 4258th SW, which was established at the new base at U-Tapao in June and began operations on 11 August. Originally intended only to serve as a base for KC-135s, U-Tapao made a contribution to the SAC effort that would grow steadily in the years to come, 'Arc Light' bomber forces arriving in April 1967 and drone and U-2 reconnaissance activities being concentrated here with effect from the summer of 1970. From mid-1966 onwards Kadena and U-Tapao served as the two main operating bases, the former concentrating mainly on supporting 'Arc Light' bomber aircraft while U-Tapao looked after 'Young Tiger' fighters. Other bases hosted KC-135s from time to time, Takhli being typical in that it was home for ten aircraft between 1965 and 1967, this small force being collectively known as 'King Cobra'. Slightly further afield, Ching Chuan Kang Air Base on Taiwan also served as a KC-135 base for some considerable time, as did Clark in the Philippines.

As the intensity of the air war fluctuated, so too did the number of Stratotankers

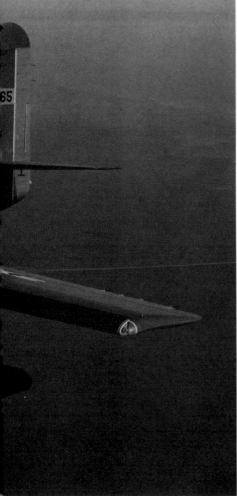

Far left: Although initially considered for the 'Arc Light' force, the Stratojet continued to be phased out during 1964–65. This particular aircraft was one of the last examples to be retired by the 9th SAW although it displayed the insignia of the 43rd BW on its nose when this photograph was taken, in memory of the days when the 43rd was stationed at Davis-Monthan. (APN)

Far left: Although perceived as being principally equipped with bomber and tanker aircraft, SAC also included a substantial number of other types in its line-up, these mainly being employed as 'hacks'. Not surprisingly, the C-47, T-29, T-33 and T-39 featured prominently, but a few examples of the Grumman HU-16B Albatross amphibian were also operated by SAC elements located in Canada, such as the 95th Strategic Wing at Goose Bay, Labrador. (Grumman)

situated in the Far East rise and fall in line with demand. By 1970, for example, the need for aerial refuelling support was probably at its lowest level since 1965, and the 30 aircraft at U-Tapao were able to satisfy most of the requirements, freeing the fifteen at Kadena for missions which were only occasionally related to the war. Less than two years later, the 1972 spring invasion of South Vietnam signalled the start of a massive build-up of US air power and, with additional tactical and bomber aircraft committed to combat, there was a commensurate need for more tanker resources. SAC was, of course, well able to satisfy this demand, and the number of KC-135s in this part of the world reached a peak of 195 as the year progressed. This remarkably high level was maintained throughout the 'Linebacker II' bombing campaign aimed at the heart of North Vietnam, although it sorely tested SAC's capability in other areas.

Tankers began returning home to the USA following the cease-fire in early 1973, but at least 100 remained in place until late summer when the US bombing of Cambodia finally came to an end. By then, in some 195,000 sorties, SAC's KC-135s had accomplished no fewer than 813,878 aerial refuellings, had transferred nearly nine billion pounds of fuel, and had been directly responsible for saving many aircraft which would otherwise have crashed. Fighter crews soon came to recognize the value of the tanker, and there were many occasions when KC-135 crews were rewarded for a 'save' with well-earned barrels of beer.

In much the same way as the size of the KC-135 fleet waxed and waned, so too did fluctuations occur within the B-52 force. For example, the decision to base the 'Buff' at U-Tapao, Thailand, in spring 1967 was largely prompted by the desire to satisfy the steadily increasing demand for this aircraft's services during the 'Arc Light' offensive. U-Tapao was situated much closer to the war zone, and missions from this base seldom lasted more than four hours compared with at least twelve from Guam. Having attained a level of 800 sorties per month in 1967, further massive increases followed early in 1968 after the hurried deployment of more B-52Ds to Kadena, this being one of several measures taken by the US within hours of the North Korean seizure of the USS *Pueblo* in January. North Vietnam's major Tet

offensive and the closely allied siege of the Marine base at Khe Sanh more or less coincided with the build-up of the B-52 force, and the Kadena-based aircraft were soon introduced to combat, successive rises to 1,200 and then to 1,800 sorties per month necessitating their involvement. This level was maintained until 1969, when a steady decline set in, the sortie rate falling in stages over the next couple of years to 1,000 per month in June 1971. This was a level that could be adequately satisfied by U-Tapao's force of 42 B-52Ds, and it remained in effect until early in 1972 when reconnaissance of the Ho Chi Minh trail revealed alarming signs of a coming enemy offensive. Once again, the sortie level began to rise, initially to 1,200 per month and then in closely spaced increments to 3,150 per month, accelerated by the massive North Vietnamese incursions of the Easter weekend and by steadily deteriorating results in the course of the ground battle.

THE BOMBING INTENSIFIES

The unprecedented level of 3,150 sorties per month was achieved in June and had been predated in April by B-52 strikes on targets in North Vietnam for the first time since the summer of 1968. However, the 42 aircraft that were already in place at U-Tapao when the first evidence of the build-up was detected were clearly inadequate to satisfy the much increased demand for B-52 support, so the deployment of additional aircraft began in February 1972 when an initial batch of 29 B-52Ds was consigned to Andersen as the first of several 'Bullet Shot' movements designed to augment the existing force. By the time 'Bullet Shot' was complete, in May, the number of Stratofortresses engaged in combat operations had risen to 200, and the B-52G was also making a contribution to the war effort for the first time.

At 50 aircraft U-Tapao's B-52 force was impressive, but at 150 aircraft Andersen's B-52 force was incredible, and gave rise to jokes that the island of Guam was in danger of sinking into the Pacific Ocean under the weight of all that 'heavy metal'. Virtually every single B-52D that could be pressed into action had been sent to South-East Asia, the 100-odd examples available being distributed more or less equally between U-Tapao and Andersen. In addition, Andersen

the course of 'Linebacker II'. It could have been worse, for roughly 1,000 SAMs were launched against the US aircraft, while MiG-21 interceptors were also known to have been active. The defending fighter forces achieved little, however, two falling victim to B-52D tail-gunners, and some 'own goals' were apparently scored when MiG-21s were shot down by their own SAMs.

Ultimately, the North Vietnamese returned to the negotiating table in Paris, a cease-fire was quickly agreed, and the bombing of the North finally ended on 15 January 1973. Raids over South Vietnam continued until 27 January when the peace agreement came into effect, but Laos and Cambodia suffered for a few months longer. In the end, the last mission over Laos was

Left: Although the B-52G was added to the combat force in 1972, it was the trusty B-52D which was the prime bomb carrier and it was hardly surprising that virtually every available example of this derivative was despatched to either U-Tapao or Andersen to take part in the intensive bombing campaign of that year. (Author)

was also crowded with just under 100 B-52Gs, and both sub-types made a vital contribution to first stalling and then reversing the North Vietnamese incursions, ranging far and wide over South Vietnam in order to do so.

With the situation in the south more or less stable again, the B-52s began to head north, completing several hundred strikes on southern North Vietnam during 'Linebacker', which terminated in late October with yet another bombing halt in the hope that a lasting truce could be obtained. As it transpired, this hope was ill-founded, and the B-52s were again pressed into action against the North in an operation codenamed 'Linebacker II'. Often referred to as the 'Eleven-Day War' and conducted in the latter half of December 1972, 'Linebacker II' took the form of an intensive and sustained aerial assault on targets in the vicinity of Hanoi and Haiphong. Just over 13,000 tons of bombs were dispensed by the B-52s in the course of 729 sorties, and the campaign was highlighted by the raid on 26 December when a force of 120 aircraft was despatched against ten targets. All 120 were due to deliver their bombs within the space of just fifteen minutes, while a further 100 aircraft from the Air Force and Navy were active in various support functions ranging from SAM-suppression to 'MiG watch'. Meticulous attention to detail was a key factor in the success of this mission, but the raid was not entirely one-sided, and two B-52s were destroyed by the defences, the last of fifteen Stratofortresses to meet their demise during

staged on 17 April, while raids on Cambodian targets continued until 15 August.

NEW EQUIPMENT

Although the war in South-East Asia tended to dominate SAC's activities throughout the latter half of the 1960s and early 1970s, the Command was no less active in other areas, nuclear deterrence still being by far the most important aspect of its work. With the B-47 now gone, the B-52 and the B-58 continued to constitute the manned bomber portion of SAC's contribution, but new equipment, in the shape of the General Dynamics FB-111A, was in prospect. This new medium bomber was selected for service with SAC in 1965, and the aircraft, originally expected to total 210, would replace the older B-52s as well as the B-58s. In the event, things did not quite turn out as planned, and a review of the programme culminated in a March 1969 statement by Secretary of Defense Melvin Laird that the number to be obtained would be unlikely to exceed 60. This figure was in many ways little more than a token gesture and one that was prompted by the desire 'to salvage what we can of work in progress', an acknowledgement that the FB-111A could no longer be perceived as an intercontinental bomber. From SAC's point of view, this decision was accompanied by a 'sweetener', for Laird's statement also directed that the development of the AMSA (Advanced Manned Strategic Aircraft) be accelerated, North American Rockwell, Boeing and

Below: Displaying SAC's star-spangled sash on the nose section and with a quartet of AGM-69A Short-Range Attack Missiles underwing, a development example of the General Dynamics FB-111A is seen here during a test flight. Procurement of the FB-111A was at one time expected to exceed 200. (Boeing)

General Dynamics all being invited to submit proposals for what was eventually given the designation B-1.

While work on the B-1 project was getting under way, SAC took delivery of the first FB-111A at Carswell AFB, Texas, on 8 October and promptly assigned it to the 340th Bomb Group at the same base. Two further aircraft had joined this unit by the end of the year, but progress was slow since the FB-111A was subjected to the same grounding orders as those brought about by accidents affecting Tactical Air Command aircraft. Tasked with conducting initial training, the 340th BG remained active until the end of 1971, by which time the two operational wings, the 380th BW at Plattsburgh AFB in New York and the 509th BW at Pease AFB in New Hampshire, had converted.

Even as the FB-111A was in the process of joining SAC, another bomber type was nearing the end of its front-line career – the B-58 Hustler. Withdrawal of the aircraft was accomplished quite swiftly, both the 43rd BW at Little Rock and the 305th BW at Grissom disposing of their aircraft in little more than ten weeks with effect from early November 1969. The retirement of the B-58 and the lengthy phasing-in of the FB-111A meant that SAC had to rely solely on the B-52 for its manned bomber deterrent throughout 1970. Even with this reliable type, change had been the order of the day during the past few years, reductions in the number of operational units having been accompanied by revised methods of deployment. Surprisingly, though, the number of aircraft which disappeared from the inventory was small, only time-expired machines being withdrawn at this time, and it was not until 1971 that major reductions in the size of the fleet occurred when the B-52C model was retired.

Ground alert still kept some 40 per cent of the bomber and tanker force – and virtually all the ICBMs – occupied, but there had been some changes in the way that this was organized as SAC again explored the virtues of dispersal in 1968–69, considering an extension of the B-47 dispersal effort of several years earlier. Part of the testing of the revised concept was entrusted to the Ramey, Puerto Rico-based 72nd BW, which began experimenting with a satellite-basing concept whereby a small number of B-52Gs and KC-135As were shifted to Homestead

AFB, Florida. Occupying quarters which had been utilized by the 19th BW until the summer of 1968, the 72nd BW machines were held on alert in a three-month test

TABLE 11: SAC ORDER OF BATTLE, DECEMBER 1970

Division	Base	Unit	Components	Equipment
2nd Air Force (Barksdale AFB, La)				
–	Altus AFB, Ok	11th ARS		KC-135A
–	Travis AFB, Ca	916th ARS		KC-135A
19th AD	Barksdale AFB, La	2nd BW	62/596 BS	B-52G
			71/913 ARS	KC-135A
	Carswell AFB, Tx	7th BW	20 BS	B-52D
			7 ARS	KC-135A
	Dyess AFB, Tx	96th SAW	337 BS	B-52D
			917 ARS	KC-135A
	Carswell AFB, Tx	340th BG	4007 CCTS	FB-111A
40th AD	Wurtsmith AFB, Mi	379th BW	524 BS	B-52H
			920 ARS	KC-135A
	K. I. Sawyer AFB, Mi	410th BW	644 BS	B-52H
			46 ARS	KC-135A
	Kincheloe AFB, Mi	449th BW	716 BS	B-52H
			908 ARS	KC-135A
42nd AD	Blytheville AFB, Ar	97th BW	340 BS	B-52G
			97 ARS	KC-135A
	Rickenbacker AFB, Oh	301st ARW	32/91 ARS	KC-135A
	Grissom AFB, In	305th ARW	70/305 ARS	KC-135A
			3 ACCS	EC-135A/G/L
45th AD	Wright-Patterson AFB, Oh	17th BW	34 BS	B-52H
			922 ARS	KC-135A
	Loring AFB, Me	42nd BW	69 BS	B-52G
			42/407 ARS	KC-135A
	Griffiss AFB, NY	416th BW	668 BS	B-52G
			41 ARS	KC-135A
	Goose Bay Airport, Labrador	95th SW	TDY	KC-135
47th AD	Castle AFB, Ca	93rd BW	328/329 BS	B-52F
			4017 CCTS	B-52F
			93/924 ARS	KC-135A
817th AD	Westover AFB, Ma	99th BW	346/348 BS	B-52C/D
			99 ARS	KC-135A
	Plattsburgh AFB, NY	380th SAW	528 BS	B-52G (preparing for FB-111A)
			310/380 ARS	KC-135A
	Pease AFB, NH	509th BW	393/715 BS	FB-111A
			34/509 ARS	KC-135A
823rd AD	Robins AFB, Ga	19th BW	28 BS	B-52G
			912 ARS	KC-135A
	Seymour-Johnson AFB, NC	68th BW	51 BS	B-52G
			911 ARS	KC-135A
	Ramey AFB, Puerto Rico	72nd BW	60 BS	B-52G
			915 ARS	KC-135A
	McCoy AFB, Fl	306th BW	367 BS	B-52D
			306/919 ARS	KC-135A
15th Air Force (March AFB, Ca)				
4th SAD	Fairchild AFB, Wa	92nd SAW	325 BS	B-52G
			43/92 ARS	KC-135A
	Grand Forks AFB, ND	319th BW	46 BS	B-52H
			905 ARS	KC-135A
	Grand Forks AFB, ND	321st SMW	446/447/448 SMS	LGM-30F Minuteman II

Continued on p. 101

project which began on 20 February 1969 and which proved to be the forerunner of more widespread introduction with effect from July of the same year.

By then, airborne alert was no longer a feature of SAC operational doctrine, this having been abandoned in 1968 largely as a result of several accidents involving B-52s engaged in this task. The first and perhaps best-known mishap occurred in January 1966 when a 68th BW B-52G collided with a KC-135A over Palomares, Spain, two of the four nuclear weapons carried by the bomber causing non-nuclear explosions on impact with the ground and another disappearing into the sea. A search for the missing weapon led to a successful retrieval in early April, but cleaning-up operations in the wake of this accident continued for several months, culminating in the removal of some 1,400 tons of soil and vegetation to a storage site in the USA. Two years later, on 21 January 1968, a 380th SAW B-52G, again with four nuclear weapons on board, crashed and burned at North Star Bay while approaching Thule AB, Greenland. On this occasion, all four 'nukes' were destroyed by fire. Tidying up continued until mid-September, by which time no less than 237,000 cubic feet of contaminated ice, snow, water and debris had been removed to the USA. Airborne alert was quietly abandoned.

MORE REORGANIZATION
Manpower reductions and a decline in the size of the force under its command eventually prompted the rationalization of SAC's organization during 1970, and this resulted in the number of ConUS-based, numbered Air Forces under SAC control falling from three to two on 31 March. Westover's 8th AF was eliminated in this reshuffle, and the accompanying reorganization led to the surviving 2nd AF henceforth being made up entirely of manned aircraft, with FB-111A, B-52 and KC-135 units under its jurisdiction. In contrast, the 15th AF was predominantly missile-orientated, although it also managed the entire strategic reconnaissance force as well as a few B-52 and KC-135 units. Further realignment took place in the first half of 1973, resulting in a far more equitable distribution of operational elements and a certain amount of diversification among the subordinate Air Divisions.

	Base	Wing	Squadron	Aircraft
12th SAD	Eielson AFB, Ak	6th SW	24 SRS TDY	RC-135 KC-135A
	Offutt AFB, Ne	55th SRW	343 SRS 2 ACCS	RC-135 EC-135C
	Davis-Monthan AFB, Az	100th SRW	349 SRS 350 SRS	U-2C/R DC-130, drones
	Davis-Monthan, AFB, Az	390th SMW	570/571 SMS	LGM-25C Titan II
14th SAD	Beale AFB, Ca	9th SRW	1/99 SRS	SR-71A/B, T-38A
	March AFB, Ca	22nd BW	2/486 BS 22/909 ARS	B-52C/D KC-135A
	Mather AFB, Ca	320th BW	441 BS 904 ARS	B-52G KC-135A
	Beale AFB, Ca	456th SAW	744 BS 9/903 ARS	B-52G KC-135A/Q
17th SAD	Little Rock AFB, Ar	308th SMW	373/374 SMS	LGM-25C Titan II
	Whiteman AFB, Mo	351st SMW	508/509/510 SMS	LGM-30F Minuteman II
	McConnell AFB, Ks	381st SMW	532/533 SMS	LGM-25C Titan II
810th SAD	Minot AFB, ND	5th BW	23 BS 906 ARS	B-52H KC-135A
	Minot AFB, ND	91st SMW	740 SMS	Converting from LGM-30B to LGM-30G
			741 SMS	LGM-30G Minuteman III
			742 SMS	LGM-30B Minuteman I
	Malmstrom AFB, Mt	341st SMW	10/12/490/564 SMS	LGM-30F Minuteman II
821st SAD	Ellsworth AFB, SD	28th BW	77 BS 28 ARS 4 ACCS	B-52D KC-135A EC-135C
	Ellsworth AFB, SD	44th SMW	66/67/68 SMS	LGM-30B Minuteman I
	F. E. Warren AFB, Wy	90th SMW	319/320/321/400 SMS	LGM-30B Minuteman I
8th Air Force (Andersen AFB, Guam)				
	Andersen AFB, Guam	43rd SW	4182 SS*	B-52, KC-135, C-97
	U-Tapao, Thailand	307th SW	4180/4181 SS*	B-52, KC-135
	Kadena AB, Okinawa	376th SW	4220 ARS, Ching Chuan Kang*	KC-135
			82 SRS	RC-135
98th Strategic Wing (Torrejon AB, Spain)				
TDY KC-135s, with detachments at other European locations, e.g. Mildenhall, UK				

*Not operational

For the 8th AF, the period in limbo was mercifully brief: within the space of twelve hours it had re-opened for business at Andersen AFB, Guam, inheriting personnel

This spread: In close to ten years of direct support of the air war in South-East Asia, SAC KC-135s accomplished no fewer than 195,000 sorties, transferring nine billion pounds of fuel in the remarkable tally of 813,878 refuellings. In the process, they also saved a large number of aircraft which would otherwise have crashed. (Author)

Left: Initial deliveries of the FB-111A coincided with the phase-out of an earlier type from the General Dynamics factory at Fort Worth. This was the B-58 Hustler, which was withdrawn in remarkably short order, 83 of the surviving aircraft being committed to storage at Davis-Monthan AFB, Arizona, between 3 November 1969 and 16 January 1970. Some of the earliest arrivals are seen here. (Author)

and missions previously assigned to the 3rd Air Division, which was itself deactivated at this time. Prompted by the desire to perpetuate a historically significant organization (the 8th AF had a particularly illustrious Second World War record), this transfer marked the start of a five-year association with combat operations in South-East Asia, during which time it grew significantly in size. Eventually, with the war effort winding down, the 8th AF returned to the USA on 1 January 1975. This time, however, it was stationed at Barksdale AFB, Louisiana, and its arrival signalled the demise of the 2nd AF which had a far less impressive historical background.

By then, with the end of the Vietnam War at least in sight, SAC was coming to terms with new weapons and laying plans for the future. Boeing's AGM-69A Short-Range Attack Missile (SRAM) was in the process of being introduced, the Loring-based 42nd BW having taken delivery of the first examples little more than a year beforehand, on 4 March 1972. Ultimately destined for delivery to all B-52G, B-52H and FB-111A units, SRAM was in some ways perceived as a penetration aid, being employed to suppress defences and permit bomber aircraft to reach and attack key targets. Nevertheless, it was – and, for that matter, still is – a powerful weapon in its own right, and its introduction greatly enhanced the B-52's

capability, for each 'Buff' could carry as many as twenty missiles, six on pylons fitted beneath each wing plus eight more on a rotary launcher contained in the bomb bay (which is capacious enough to accommodate four gravity weapons at the same time). FB-111s may operate with a maximum of six SRAMs, two in the internal weapons bay and four more underwing, and the new B-1B is also compatible with this weapon.

Indeed, it was the latter bomber, in its B-1A version, which was at the heart of SAC's hopes for the future. Rockwell and General Electric had been awarded development contracts during June 1970, Rockwell as prime contractor for the airframe and its associated systems and General Electric having responsibility for the propulsion system. The initial contract called for the manufacture of seven prototypes. Five of these were to be assigned to flight test duties while the other two were allocated for static and fatigue testing. In the event, the first of many changes which were to plague the B-1 occurred in February 1971 when the number of flyable prototypes on order was cut to just three. Nevertheless, with flight testing of Rockwell's bomber set to begin in mid-1974, SAC was optimistic that its fortunes were about to take a turn for the better. With the benefit of hindsight, it is now clear that their optimism was a little premature . . .

Right: Even though the bomber force had contracted drastically during the course of the 1960s, 'confidence remained high', largely as a result of the anticipated availability of new weaponry like Boeing's AGM-69A Short-Range Attack Missile (SRAM), which was introduced to service on the B-52Gs of the 42nd Bomb Wing in 1972. (Boeing)

Overleaf: The cornerstone around which SAC's hopes for the future were built in the early 1970s, Rockwell's B-1A is almost engulfed by the crowd on the occasion of its roll-out at Palmdale. This attractive bomber suffered its fair share of controversy before it was eventually cancelled by the Carter administration in 1977. (Rockwell)

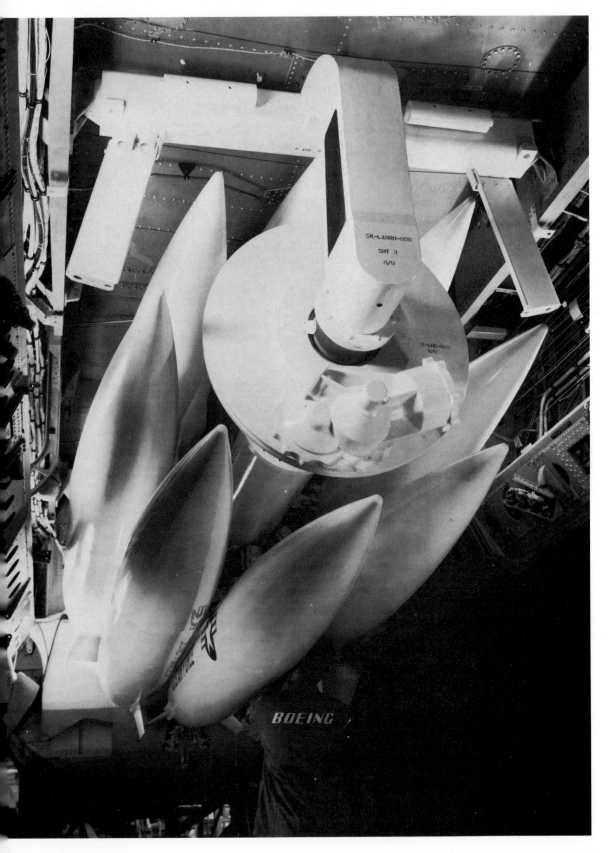

THE POST-VIETNAM ERA

Since the end of the Vietnam War Strategic Air Command has faced further decline in quantitative terms, the effects of this perhaps having been felt most keenly by the manned bomber force and, to a lesser extent, by the tanker squadrons. To comprehend more fully the reduction in size which has occurred over the past decade or so, it is worth taking a few moments to consider the strength of the Command as it was shortly after the end of hostilities. At that time, as indeed it still is today, SAC's premier bomber in terms of numbers was the Stratofortress, some 420 examples being distributed between 22 US-based Bomb Wings and the sole overseas-based unit on

Guam. Variants in use comprised the B-52D, B-52F, B-52G and B-52H, and although each of the four sub-types was capable of delivering nuclear weapons, the primary responsibility for deterrence rested with about 275 B-52Gs and B-52Hs which had been modified to carry up to twenty AGM-69A SRAMs in addition to free-fall bombs. The older B-52D was also called upon to stand nuclear alert duty as a matter of routine, but this aircraft was less flexible in that it could carry only gravity devices; as a consequence, virtually all the 120 or so B-52Ds that remained active were tasked principally with waging conventional war.

Even though the B-52D was now nearing

"Progress without Fear or Prejudice' – motto of the 11th Air Refueling Wing

Below: Ranking as one of the most feared weapons of the entire Vietnam War, the B-52D was showing signs of age by the beginning of the 1970s and duly became the subject of extensive modernization efforts aimed at extending service life. (USAF)

vintage status, SAC readily acknowledged that the conventional bombing capability of this sub-type was unsurpassed and the Command was therefore anxious to retain it on the inventory for the foreseeable future. However, since most of the B-52Ds had been subjected to the rigours of combat, many of the airframes were 'tired' and in need of urgent rejuvenation. 'Pacer Plank' accomplished just that objective between 1972 and 1977, this five-year programme of fuselage and wing strengthening costing $219 million; for that outlay, SAC ended up with a fleet of 80 aircraft with a projected service life extending to the beginning of the next century. Most of the unmodified machines were retained for a few more years, distributed amongst other SAC wings and employed in training duties before finally being retired in the latter half of 1978. The only other Stratofortress model still in SAC service in 1973 was the B-52F, about 20 examples of which were assigned to the 93rd BW at Castle AFB, California. Crew training was their major mission, the 93rd being unique in that it also possessed a number of B-52Gs and B-52Hs to introduce personnel to the variant that they would fly following their posting to an operational unit. The bomber forces were completed by the two FB-111A wings situated in the north-east, some 70 aircraft being on hand at the end of 1973. Limited with regard to the amount of armament that it could carry, the FB-111A nevertheless packed a respectable punch, and was compatible with both SRAM and gravity weapons; indeed, it was probably rather better suited to the penetration mission, its small size, high speed and infinitely superior terrain-following capability making the aircraft hard to destroy.

SAC still possessed an extremely large fleet of KC-135 tankers, well over 600 being on charge in 1973. Virtually all the bomber units numbered at least one assigned tanker squadron amongst their assets, while a few (such as the FB-111A-equipped 380th and 509th BWs) had two. In addition, a handful of dedicated air refuelling units existed, as typified by the 307th Air Refueling Group at Travis AFB, California, which had one KC-135 squadron assigned (the 916th ARS), and the 384th Air Refueling Wing at McConnell AFB, Kansas, with two (the 91st and 384th ARSs). SAC's three principal types of reconnaissance aircraft were distributed among

TABLE 12: SAC ORDER OF BATTLE, AUTUMN 1978

Division	Base	Unit	Components	Equipment
8th Air Force (Barksdale AFB, La)				
19th AD (Carswell AFB, Tx)				
	Barksdale AFB, La	2nd BW	62/596 BS	B-52G
			71/913 ARS	KC-135A
	Carswell AFB, Tx	7th BW	9/20 BS	B-52D
			4018 CCTS	B-52D
			7 ARS	KC-135A
	Altus AFB, Ok	340th ARG	11 ARS	KC-135A
	McConnell AFB, Ks	381st SMW	532/533 SMS	LGM-25C Titan II
	McConnell AFB, Ks	384th ARW	91/384 ARS	KC-135A
40th AD (Wurtsmith AFB, Mi)				
	Grissom AFB, In	305th ARW	70 ARS	KC-135A, EC-135A/G/L
			305 ARS	KC-135A
	Whiteman AFB, Mo	351st SMW	508/509/510 SMS	LGM-30F Minuteman II
	Wurtsmith AFB, Mi	379th BW	524 BS	B-52H
			920 ARS	KC-135A
	K. I. Sawyer AFB, Mi	410th BW	644 BS	B-52H
			46 ARS	KC-135A
42nd AD (Blytheville AFB, Ar)				
	Robins AFB, Ga	19th BW	28 BS	B-52G
			912 ARS	KC-135A
	Seymour-Johnson AFB, NC	68th BW	51 BS	B-52G
			911 ARS	KC-135A
	Blytheville AFB, Ar	97th BW	340 BS	B-52G
			97 ARS	KC-135A
	Rickenbacker AB, Oh	301st ARW	32 ARS	KC-135A
	Little Rock AFB, Ar	308th SMW	373/374 SMS	LGM-25C Titan II
45th AD (Pease AFB, NH)				
	Loring AFB, Me	42nd BW	69 BS	B-52G
			42/407 ARS	KC-135A
	Plattsburgh AFB, NY	380th BW	528/529 BS	FB-111A
			4007 CCTS	FB-111A
			310/380 ARS	KC-135A/Q
	Griffiss AFB, NY	416th BW	668 BS	B-52G
			41 ARS	KC-135A
	Pease AFB, NH	509th BW	393/715 BS	FB-111A
			509 ARS	KC-135A
15th Air Force (March AFB, Ca)				
4th AD (F. E. Warren AFB, Wy)				
	Ellsworth AFB, SD	28th BW	37/77 BS	B-52H
			28 ARS	KC-135A
			4 ACCS	EC-135C
	Ellsworth AFB, SD	44th SMW	66/67/68 SMS	LGM-30F Minuteman II
	Offutt AFB, Ne	55th SRW	1 ACCS	E-4A
			2 ACCS	EC-135C
			343 SRS	RC-135
	F. E. Warren AFB, Wy	90th SMW	319/320/321/400 SMS	LGM-30G Minuteman III
12th AD (Dyess AFB, Tx)				
	March AFB, Ca	22nd BW	2 BS	B-52D
			22 ARS	KC-135A
	Dyess AFB, Tx	96th BW	337 BS	B-52D
			917 ARS	KC-135A
	Davis-Monthan AFB, Az	390th SMW	570/571 SMS	LGM-25C Titan II

Continued on p. 109

three wings, the 9th SRW at Beale operating about a dozen SR-71As, the 55th SRW at Offutt equipped with RC-135 'ferrets' of various extensively modified sub-types and the 100th SRW at Davis-Monthan utilizing the surviving U-2s. Two semi-independent Strategic Reconnaissance Squadrons also existed, these being the 24th SRS at Eielson, Alaska, and the 82nd SRS at Kadena, Okinawa; reporting respectively to the 6th SW and the 376th SW, these units also operated various RC-135s. The only other aircraft-operating elements were responsible for the airborne command posts (ACPs) which constituted the Post Attack Command Control System. Three squadrons were engaged in this vital task; all flew EC-135s, Offutt's 2nd Airborne Command and Control Squadron being the premier unit in that it was responsible for 'Looking Glass'. Other elements in the PACCS network comprised the 3rd ACCS at Grissom AFB, Indiana, and the 4th ACCS at Ellsworth AFB, North Dakota.

With regard to ICBMs, there had been little change as far as organization was concerned, SAC capability in this area still resting with its six Minuteman and three Titan II Strategic Missile Wings. As detailed elsewhere, however, the ICBM force was by no means static in terms of its capability, efforts aimed at modernizing various facets of the Minuteman system being pursued vigorously until well into the 1970s.

B-52 RETIREMENTS
In the ensuing decade, rationalization, the

14th AD (Beale AFB, Ca)			
Beale AFB, Ca	9th SRW	1 SRS	SR-71A/B/C
		99 SRS	U-2C/CT/R
Castle AFB, Ca	93rd BW	328 BS	B-52G/H
		4017 CCTS	B-52G/H
		93/924 ARS	KC-135A
Beale AFB, Ca	100th ARW	9/349 ARS	KC-135Q
Travis AFB, Ca	307th ARG	916 ARS	KC-135A
Mather AFB, Ca	320th BW	441 BS	B-52G
		904 ARS	KC-135A
47th AD (Fairchild AFB, Wa)			
Eielson AFB, Ak	6th SW	24 SRS	RC-135 (TDY KC-135A also present)
Fairchild AFB, Wa	92nd BW	325 BS	B-52G
		43/92 ARS	KC-135A
Malmstrom AFB, Mt	341st SMW	10/12/490 SMS	LGM-30F Minuteman II
		564 SMS	LGM-30G Minuteman III
57th AD (Minot AFB, ND)			
Minot AFB, ND	5th BW	23 BS	B-52H
		906 ARS	KC-135A
Minot AFB, ND	91st SMW	740/741/742 SMS	LGM-30G Minuteman III
Grand Forks AFB, ND	319th BW	46 BS	B-52H
		905 ARS	KC-135A
Grand Forks AFB, ND	321st SMW	446/447/448 SMS	LGM-30G Minuteman III
3rd AD (Andersen AFB, Guam)			
Andersen AFB, Guam	43rd SW	60 BS	B-52D (TDY tankers also present)
Kadena AB, Okinawa	376th SW	909 ARS	KC-135A/Q
7th AD (Ramstein AB, West Germany)			
RAF Mildenhall, UK	306th SW		TDY tanker aircraft

Left: The distinctive 'thimble' nose and prominent side-looking airborne radar fairings on the fuselage sides help to identify this as one of the four RC-135D conversions. Based on standard KC-135As, these aircraft were amongst the first of the Stratotanker 'ferrets' to appear. (Author)

transfer of some aircraft and the desire to phase out older variants of the B-52 inevitably led to a sizeable reduction in quantitative terms, although this has to some extent been compensated for by the introduction of new weapons and, more recently, new aircraft such as the KC-10 and the B-1B. Significant reductions in the size of the B-52 force were made during the latter half of 1978 when some 60 B-52Ds and B-52Fs were despatched for storage, although, rather surprisingly, this had little impact on the number of units which remained active, most of the machines that were sent to Davis-Monthan at this time having been employed as training aids. The strength of the force thereafter remained fairly constant until about 1982, when the retirement of the 80 or so B-52Ds that were still operational began in earnest. By 1984 the phasing out had been more or less completed, but a realignment exercise that ran concurrently

meant that not all of the B-52D units disappeared.

Of the four wings which had used the B-52D model, only one, the 22nd BW at March AFB, California, ceased to operate the Stratofortress immediately; even then the disposal of the 'Buff' was not accompanied by deactivation, the 22nd instead acquiring the McDonnell Douglas KC-10A Extender and being redesignated an Air Refueling Wing. Two of the other three wings involved in phasing out the B-52D were allocated B-52Hs in the reshuffle that took place, these being the 7th BW at Carswell and the 96th BW at Dyess, although the latter was destined to enjoy only a brief association with this version for it soon began to prepare for the B-1B. Finally, the 43rd SW at Andersen turned to the B-52G. Aircraft made available to those units which re-equipped were transferred in a complex realignment programme which

Above: Steadily increasing demand for in-flight refuelling support of other commands led to the decision to obtain a tanker based on an existing wide-bodied transport aircraft, either the Boeing 747 or the McDonnell-Douglas DC-10. The purchase of about sixteen examples of the victorious contender was originally anticipated, but subsequent re-orders have raised the number of KC-10A Extenders to be procured to no fewer than sixty. This example displays the insignia of the Barksdale-based 2nd Bomb Wing on the fuselage. (Author)

culminated in the deactivation of one of the 28th BW's two bomb squadrons as well as the disappearance of the 19th and 68th BWs at Robins and Seymour-Johnson respectively. With the B-52D gone, the distribution of the remaining two models then settled down for a while. However, it would seem reasonable to anticipate further changes in the near future as more and more B-1Bs join SAC, since all but one of the four units earmarked to operate the Rockwell bomber are currently equipped with either the B-52G or B-52H.

The KC-135 tanker force also suffered quite a sizeable cut in strength during the latter half of the 1970s when no fewer than 128 aircraft were reassigned to second-line elements of the Air National Guard (ANG) and the Air Force Reserve (AFRES). Plans to implement this programme were revealed in the summer of 1974, and it duly got under way on 18 April 1975 when the Rickenbacker-based 301st ARS turned over the first example to the 145th Air Refueling Squadron, an element of the Ohio ANG which shared the same base. Over the next four years twelve further ANG squadrons followed suit, as did three AFRES units, each of the sixteen squadrons involved having a unit establishment of eight aircraft.

In the normal course of events, these tankers conform to standard ANG and AFRES command practices, although it

Below: Boeing's long-serving KC-135 Strato-tanker remains the most important tanker aircraft in pure numerical terms, but SAC's fleet was the subject of a sizeable reduction in the mid-1970s when 128 aircraft were turned over to second-line units of the Air National Guard and Air Force Reserve. KC-135A 59-1509 of the New Hampshire ANG's 133rd Air Refueling Squadron, seen here refuelling a New Jersey ANG F-106A Delta Dart, is typical of the aircraft involved, although it should be noted that all 128 have been re-engined with JT3D-3B turbofans taken from redundant civil airliners and are now known as KC-135Es. (Author)

should be noted that they are what is defined as 'SAC gained', which means that, in the event of mobilization, they would automatically constitute part of SAC's forces. Peacetime training reflects this, since ANG and AFRES tanker crews are expected to achieve identical levels of performance to the regular force and each unit makes a modest contribution to the ground alert force by keeping one aircraft on standby at all times. More recently, all 128 Reserve tankers have been re-engined with the Pratt & Whitney JT3D-3B turbofan, which, while not quite as good as the CFM56 of the KC-135R, nonetheless bestows significant performance benefits, particularly with regard to field performance and fuel off-load. The aircraft, which are now known as KC-135Es, were modified from 1982, beginning with Arizona's 197th ARS.

CHANGES AT BEALE

Rationalization also extended to the strategic reconnaissance assets. After many years at Davis-Monthan, the U-2 fleet finally moved to new quarters at Beale in the summer of 1976 so as to concentrate high-altitude reconnaissance elements under the control of the 9th SRW. While this transfer was being effected, the 100th SRW remained at Davis-Monthan until the autumn, when it too moved to Beale, simultaneously being redesignated an air refuelling wing and assuming the responsibility for furnishing tanker support to the 9th's SR-71s. New equipment in the shape of the specialist KC-135Q accompanied this change of mission, and the 100th ARW continued to perform this task until it was finally eliminated in the early 1980s when the two tanker squadrons reverted to 9th SRW control.

Change was also evident with the Post Attack Command Control System, Grissom's 3rd ACCS being deactivated in 1975 when the responsibility for that unit's radio relay aspect of the mission passed to the 70th ARS at the same base. However, the number of airborne command post squadrons remained unchanged, for SAC acquired the Boeing E-4 National Emergency Airborne Command Post (NEACP) aircraft – perhaps better known as 'Kneecap' – at around the same time. Then based at Andrews and originally part of Headquarters Command, the 1st ACCS eventually

moved to Offutt and joined up with the rest of the 55th SRW in 1977, its E-4s subsequently fulfilling SAC's own 'Looking Glass' mission as well as NEACP duty. To undertake the latter, a forward operating location was established at Andrews in December 1977 so as to be close to the National Command Authorities in Washington. Just over two years later, the even more sophisticated E-4B entered service, the three original E-4As eventually being retrospectively brought to this later standard.

Today, SAC maintains a high proportion of its forces on alert, ready to take flight within a matter of minutes should the decision to execute the Emergency War Order (EWO) ever be taken. In a thousand holes scattered throughout the mid-western states, ICBMs stand idle awaiting the electrical impulses that will signal a modern-day Armageddon. As it has done for the last 30 years, the B-52 continues to do its fair share of alert duty, armed aircraft sitting quietly at dispersal close to the runway, from where they can get airborne with the minimum of delay; so, too, does a proportion of the still large KC-135 fleet. RC-135s still perform their often dangerous work of probing and assessing enemy capabilities in near anonymity, aircraft of this type going about their task with the minimum of fuss while their more glamorous reconnaissance-dedicated counterparts, the SR-71s, still tend to steal whatever headlines there are to be had. Even the veteran U-2 is still a very important element of SAC's strength, although the aircraft now in service are rather different beasts from those which joined the Command back in the mid-1950s.

PERIOD OF TRANSITION

From the foregoing, one could perhaps be excused for thinking that SAC has not changed very much in the past twenty years; after all, the Minuteman and the B-52 still constitute the backbone of retaliatory power today and, taken at face value, this would certainly seem to indicate that little progress had been made. Looking more closely, though, one soon realizes that the Command has undergone tremendous change over this period, and nowhere is this more obvious than with the B-52, which, like the U-2, has been transformed to a point where it now bears little more than a superficial resemblance to the aircraft

which originally entered service. Then the 'Buff' was basically little more than an extremely large bomb carrier intended to penetrate to its target at high level; now it operates 'down amongst the weeds', and while it may still safely be described as a bomb carrier *par excellence* it has acquired an impressive array of new sensors and weapons which have enabled the aircraft to remain a viable and effective element of the US's strategic arsenal for more than 30 years. Minuteman, too, has benefited from updating initiatives, improvements to the re-entry vehicles having been matched by a 'hardening' of the silos and the updating of associated software which permits re-target-ing to be achieved by electronic means in only a fraction of the time it once took.

Clearly, then, while SAC has been forced to retain older weapons systems on the inventory for perhaps rather longer than it would have liked, the Command has certainly not stagnated. Now, at last, new aircraft and missiles are becoming available, led by Rockwell's B-1B bomber and the Peacekeeper ICBM. Both these systems are currently operational, although the B-1B has been the subject of some recent concern over deficiencies in its integral Offensive Avionics Suite, which equipment will be vital if the bomber is ever called upon to operate in anger. Looking to the future, SAC

seems certain to acquire even more sophisticated hardware in the shapes of the Advanced Technology Bomber (ATB) and the Small ICBM, the development of both of which is, by all accounts, forging ahead at a rapid rate. However, these weapons are not expected to enter service until the early part of the next decade.

Today, SAC is quite clearly on the threshold of a major period of transition, extending to virtually all areas of endeavour. As is now usual, new technology seems to be the driving force behind the changes currently being implemented, and nowhere is this impact being more keenly felt than in the manned bomber force, which is still in the process of adapting not only to new and ever more sophisticated weaponry but also to new operational doctrine. Until just a few years ago the B-52 was viewed primarily as a penetrator, it being necessary for the aircraft physically to enter enemy territory in order to accomplish its mission of delivering nuclear weapons, be they guided missiles or gravity bombs. It was this requirement to penetrate which was largely responsible for the inclusion of the new offensive avionics equipment that is now deemed necessary if an intruding aircraft is to survive long enough to be able to press home its attack. Such updating does not come cheaply, of course, and many thousands of millions of

Below: Dwarfing the KC-135A from which it is receiving fuel, this is one of four Boeing E-4A National Emergency Airborne Command Post aircraft operated by the 55th SRW from Offutt and Andrews. The E-4A is a dual-mission aircraft in that it can perform either the NEACP mission or SAC's own 'Looking Glass' ACP duty. (Boeing)

Left: Changing times bring changing weapons: Boeing's AGM-86B Air Launched Cruise Missile will be instrumental in permitting the now ageing B-52 Stratofortress to switch from a penetrator to a stand-off weapon system and is also to be deployed aboard the newest bomber to enter service, the Rockwell B-1B. (Boeing)

dollars have been invested in the B-52 over the years. Now, however, attitudes are changing, and the B-52 is in the process of modification from a penetrator to a stand-off bomber. The key to this change is Boeing's AGM-86 Air-Launched Cruise Missile. Introduced to service on the B-52Gs of the 416th BW at Griffiss AFB, New York, and attaining an initial operational capability in December 1982, ALCM has a range that is apparently sufficient to permit about 85 per cent of the Soviet targets judged to be strategically significant to be attacked without the need to penetrate.

'SHOOT AND PENETRATE'

Even though it was becoming evident that the B-52 was much less likely to survive in an increasingly hostile and capable defence environment, in the absence of a new bomber the so-called 'shoot and penetrate' doctrine gained acceptance. As it so clearly implies, this essentially called for ALCM-configured aircraft to launch wing-mounted missiles from a position well outside enemy territory before pressing on to deliver the gravity weapons housed in the internal bomb bay, presumably against those targets which lay beyond ALCM's reach. Since each

Below: Currently, war plans anticipate employing the Strato-fortress in the 'shoot and penetrate' mode, orbiting B-52s dispos-ing of underwing ALCMs before enter-ing hostile air space to deliver either SRAM or conventional gravity nuclear weapons. Underwing stowage of ALCM is effected by a very neat pylon, as can be seen on this depart-ing B-52G. (Boeing)

B-52 may carry a maximum of twelve ALCMs underwing, 'shoot and penetrate' significantly enhanced the deterrent value of Boeing's veteran. At the time that ALCM was introduced to service, it was intended to equip only the B-52G model with this weapon, but, following the election of President Reagan, this programme was reviewed. Perhaps the most important change arising from the review was the decision to deploy ALCM on the B-52H with effect from 1985, and it now looks as if around 200 Stratofortresses will eventually carry either the AGM-86B or an even more advanced type of cruise missile now under development. At present, ALCM is confined to underwing carriage, but a new universal rotary launcher is in prospect for internal stowage in the weapons bay, and this will be able to accommodate either eight ALCMs or eight SRAMs. The availability of the new launcher should also bring about the final change in operational doctrine, and B-52s armed with ALCM will then be used solely as stand-off bombers. In this mode of operation, they will orbit outside enemy territory while launching missiles, leaving the more hazardous task of penetrating to deliver weapons to the B-1B and, with effect from the early 1990s, Northrop's ATB.

NUMERICAL SUPERIORITY

At the moment, the B-52 still occupies a position of numerical superiority in SAC's bomber force, approximately 265 remaining active. The introduction of the B-1B will almost certainly have some impact on the distribution of these aircraft, but it is not yet clear quite how SAC will organize its B-52 resources in years to come. One dozen wings are still equipped with the 'Buff', all except one being home-based within the confines of the continental USA. Only two sub-types are still to be found on the operational inventory, the B-52G (about 170 aircraft) and the B-52H (95), and these have assumed an ever greater number of missions in recent years. Evidence of this proliferation is provided by the fact that McDonnell Douglas AGM-84A Harpoon-armed aircraft of the 42nd BW at Loring, Maine, and the 43rd SW at Andersen, Guam, now specialize in long-range maritime operations, while other B-52Gs (most notably from the Barksdale-based 2nd BW) are regularly called upon to practise con-

ventional bombing, aircraft from this unit periodically visiting European bases for NATO exercises under the code name 'Busy Brewer'. The General Dynamics FB-111A still features in the operational fleet, but attrition has taken its toll over the years and only about 60 aircraft now serve with the 380th BW at Plattsburgh and the 509th BW at Pease. These are expected to be retained on SAC's inventory for a little longer, although it is intended ultimately to reassign them to Tactical Air Command.

ENTER THE B-1B

Arguably the most exciting development in the bomber field, though, has been the advent of the B-1B. Exactly 100 aircraft of this type are on order for service with SAC, and deployment began in late June 1985 when the first example was handed over to the 96th BW at Dyess AFB, Texas. This unit achieved initial operational capability with fifteen aircraft more or less on schedule in the autumn of 1986, and the first aircraft was put on alert shortly before the end of that year. Expected to have an eventual complement of 29 aircraft, the 96th BW controls the activities of a training squadron (the 4018th CCTS) and an operational squadron (the 337th BS), resources being divided roughly equally between the two. The delivery of the first aircraft earmarked for the second unit, the Ellsworth-based 28th BW, was due to take place just before the end of 1986, and the two squadrons of this wing will eventually operate a fleet of 35 B-1Bs, including three reserve aircraft. Thereafter, attention will switch to Grand Forks AFB, North Dakota, where the 319th BW is due to receive its first B-1B in August 1987, the programme terminating with the 384th BW at McConnell AFB, Kansas. This unit is scheduled to start being equipped in January 1988 and, if everything goes according to plan, the programme should be completed on the last day of April 1988. Like the 319th BW, the 384th will have a complement of seventeen aircraft, including one reserve.

Updating has by no means been confined to bomber aircraft, for SAC is also taking delivery of long-overdue new tankers in the shape of the multi-mission McDonnell Douglas KC-10A Extender, while the re-engining of the Stratotanker with the 22,000lb s.t. General Electric/

Right: Photographed while attending the Tiger Meet during one of its rare forays to Europe, this General Dynamics FB-111A acquired non-standard 'tiger' stripes across its fin in recognition of the fact that the 393rd BS, 509th BW (normally resident at Pease), features this ferocious feline in its badge.

Right: The massive in-flight refuelling boom of the KC-10A Extender is seen in the stowed position on this aircraft of the 22nd Air Refueling Wing at March AFB, California. Production of the KC-10 is now slowing down, most of the 60 examples on order having been delivered to the 2nd BW at Barksdale, the 22nd ARW at March and the 68th ARW at Seymour-Johnson. (Author)

SNECMA F108-CF-100 turbofan, in conjunction with the reskinning of the lower wing surfaces, has given this elder statesman a new lease of life. Modified aircraft are known as KC-135Rs, and the upgraded variant began to enter service with the McConnell-based 384th ARW in July 1984. Since then, several other units, including the 28th BW, have acquired the KC-135R, and SAC intends to bring a substantial proportion of its fleet of Stratotankers to this configuration. In the meantime, of course, the older J57 turbojet engine continues to power most Stratotankers, variants in use with SAC comprising the KC-135A, KC-135D and KC-135Q. Some 30 squadrons still operate Boeing's tanker, all bar one located within the continental USA. Tankers do still frequently deploy to overseas bases for periods of temporary duty, however, and this method of operation is perhaps most evident in the United Kingdom, where two bases, Fairford and Mildenhall, host continuously rotating tanker task forces. While present in the UK, command jurisdiction is exercised by the 7th Air Division via the 306th Strategic Wing (at Mildenhall) and the 11th Strategic Group (at Fairford). Other locations which regularly support KC-135 aircraft include Andersen AFB in Guam, Keflavik in Iceland, Riyadh in Saudi Arabia and Zaragoza in Spain.

IMPRESSIVE PAYLOAD

Based on the commercial DC-10 Series 30CF, the KC-10A Extender joined SAC in the spring of 1981 when the first example was delivered to the 2nd BW at Barksdale AFB, Louisiana. Original planning anticipated only modest procurement, but a subsequent revision has resulted in further orders and it now seems likely that production will eventually total 60, the aircraft being distributed among the 2nd BW, the 22nd ARW at March and the 68th ARW at Seymour-Johnson; AFRES units at these bases will provide additional air crews to man the aircraft in an extension of the highly successful 'associate' programme pioneered in conjunction with Military Airlift Command.

Capable of airlifting an impressive payload or of dispensing vast amounts of fuel, the KC-10A has been a welcome addition to SAC's assets and may now be considered a 'combat veteran', having played a key role in 'El Dorado Canyon', the April 1986 attack on a number of Libyan targets by UK-based F-111Fs and carrier aircraft of the Navy's 6th Fleet. SAC's support of this operation was spearheaded by the KC-10, no fewer than 24 aircraft assembling at Fairford and Mildenhall in the days immediately preceding the strike. Most of these played some part in the ensuing activity, as did UK-based KC-135s, TR-1s and SR-71s. Needless to say, RC-135V and RC-135W 'ferrets' from the 55th SRW were also observed in transit through the UK during the period of preparation, intelligence gleaned by these aircraft probably being of assistance in the largely successful prosecution of the attack which followed.

STRATEGIC RECONNAISSANCE

Reconnaissance activities generally have seen a modest growth during recent years, principally arising from the deployment of the TR-1. Essentially little more than a revamped U-2R, the TR-1 is, however, concerned mainly with tactical missions, hence the fact that most of the examples to be built will be stationed at Alconbury in England with the 17th Reconnaissance Wing. Employing pod-mounted and other sensors to obtain data pertaining to the enemy's electronic order of battle, the first TR-1 arrived at Alconbury in early 1983 and it seems likely that the 17th RW's eventual complement will be of the order of a dozen to eighteen, a small number of aircraft (including both the two-seat TR-1B trainers) being retained at Beale.

For long viewed as SAC's élite reconnaissance unit, the 9th has grown in size in recent years, largely by virtue of having regained responsibility for its own tanker support following the demise of the 100th ARW and the transfer of that unit's two KC-135Q squadrons, the 349th and 350th ARSs. The SR-71 'Blackbird' still provides the most spectacular evidence of this unit's elevated status, but barely ten aircraft are now active with the 1st SRS, this total including one SR-71B trainer. Extensive use is made of overseas operating locations, primarily with Detachment One at Kadena and Detachment Four at Mildenhall. Other wing elements comprise the 99th SRS and the 4029th SRTS. The former manages the small number of U-2R aircraft that remain in regular use and, once again, forward operat-

Far left: Despite the fact that the basic design is now more than 30 years old, Boeing's Stratotanker is expected to remain in everyday use with SAC until well into the twenty-first century. This is a 19th ARW KC-135R. (C. Ryan)
Below: Employed to gather data on a potential enemy's electronic order of battle, the TR-1 is the latest manifestation of Lockheed's U-2. The prominent 'superpods' house much of the mission-related avionics. (Lockheed-California)

Left: Part of the interior of a 'Looking Glass' EC-135C during its never-ending mission. In the foreground is the General Officer who heads the battle staff, members of which can be seen in the background at some of the extensive array of equipment carried by these aircraft. (USAF)

Below: Post-production modification of the Boeing E-4A led to the advent of the E-4B, the most visible evidence of change being the prominent fairing above the forward fuselage. Packed with sophisticated communications equipment, the four E-4Bs are still assigned to the 55th SRW at Offutt AFB, Nebraska, and may perform in either the NEACP or 'Looking Glass' capacity. (Boeing)

50125

ing locations feature strongly in routine activity, these including Detachment Two at Osan, Korea, Detachment Three at Akrotiri, Cyprus, and Detachment Five at Patrick AFB, Florida. As its designation implies, the 4029th Strategic Reconnaissance Training Squadron is more concerned with non-operational tasks, furnishing support to the expanding TR-1 fleet and employing both the TR-1Bs as training aids.

Another unit which frequently deploys aircraft to overseas locations is the 55th SRW at Offutt AFB, although this wing's mission is by no means confined to strategic reconnaissance since it also has responsibility for SAC's 'Looking Glass' airborne command post and for 'Kneecap'. Reconnaissance does, however, constitute a major part of the 55th SRW's activities, and the much-modified RC-135U, RC-135V and RC-135W aircraft naturally range far and wide in their efforts to 'ferret out' electronic intelligence. Two of the wing's four squadrons are dedicated to this task, the 38th SRS providing pilots and navigators to fly the RC-135s and the 343rd SRS consisting of electronic warfare officers (EWOs) with responsibility for managing the impressive array of kit carried by these aircraft. SAC's strategic reconnaissance force is completed by the 24th SRS at Eielson AFB, Alaska. Assigned to the 6th Strategic Wing, this unit also operates diverse RC-135s from Eielson and from Shemya to obtain electronic intelligence on Soviet facilities in this area.

PACCS

Returning to the 55th SRW, the second major mission performed by this unit concerns SAC's Post Attack Command and Control System, a task carried out by a fleet of EC-135Cs and E-4Bs in conjunction with other elements stationed at Ellsworth and Grissom. Boeing's E-4B may actually fulfil the dual functions of SAC airborne command post ('Looking Glass') and NEACP, and the 55th SRW does maintain a permanent forward operating location at Andrews AFB to satisfy the latter requirement, personnel coming from the 1st ACCS which actually 'owns' the E-4Bs. Most of the 1960s-vintage EC-135Cs are assigned to the 2nd ACCS and are dedicated to PACCS, other key components comprising alternative ACPs at Ellsworth with the 4th ACCS and EC-135G/L aircraft with the 70th ARS at

TABLE 13: SAC ORDER OF BATTLE, 1987			
Unit	Base	Components	Equipment
2nd BW	Barksdale, La	62/596 BS	B-52G
		32 ARS	KC-10A
		71 ARS	KC-135A
5th BW	Minot, ND	23 BS	B-52H
		906 ARS	KC-135A
6th SW	Eielson, Ak	24 SRS	RC-135S/T (Det. at Shemya; also hosts TDY KC-135s)
7th BW	Carswell, Tx	9/20 BS	B-52H
		7 ARS	KC-135A
9th SRW	Beale, Ca'	1 SRS	SR-71A, T-38A
		4029 SRTS	TR-1B, SR-71B/C, T-38A, U-2CT
		99 SRS	TR-1A, U-2R
		349/350 ARS	KC-135Q
11th SG	RAF Fairford	TDY	KC-135A
17th RW	RAF Alconbury	95 RS	TR-1A
19th ARW	Robins, Ga	99/912 ARS	KC-135R
22nd ARW	March, Ca	9 ARS	KC-10A
		22 ARS	KC-135A
28th BW	Ellsworth, SD	37/77 BS	Receiving B-1B
		28 ARS	KC-135R
		4 ACCS	EC-135A/C/G
42nd BW	Loring, Me	69 BS	B-52G
		42/407 ARS	KC-135A
43rd SW	Andersen, Guam	60 BS	B-52G (TDY KC-135A)
44th SMW	Ellsworth, SD	66/67/68 SMS	LGM-30F
55th SRW	Offutt, Ne	1 ACCS	E-4B
		2 ACCS	EC-135C
		38/343 SRS	RC-135U/V/W, KC-135
68th ARW	Seymour-Johnson, NC	344/911 ARS	KC-10A
90th SMW	F. E. Warren, Wy	319/320/321 SMS	LGM-30G
		400 SMS	MGM-118A
91st SMW	Minot, ND	740/741/742 SMS	LGM-30G

Continued on p. 125

Grissom, the latter being employed mainly on radio relay duties. Although one 'Looking Glass' EC-135C is kept aloft at all times, PACCS actually requires the services of no fewer than eight aircraft if it is to function efficiently. The primary SAC airborne command post and the East Auxiliary Command Post are both provided from 1st or 2nd ACCS resources at Offutt, while the West Auxiliary Command Post and three Airborne Launch Control Centers with the capability to send ICBMs on their way are assigned to Ellsworth's 4th ACCS. Finally, the responsibility for the two radio relay platforms which form part of PACCS is entrusted to the 70th ARS. Needless to say, the entire organization is periodically exer-

Right: Seen getting airborne from Mildenhall at the start of another mission, the Lockheed SR-71A still ranks as one of SAC's key intelligence-gathering tools and looks likely to continue flying with the 9th SRW for the foreseeable future. (Author)

cised under conditions which duplicate as closely as possible those that would obtain in a 'real' situation.

FACING THE FUTURE

Change is also much in evidence in the ICBM 'fields', and the long-serving Titan II should have disappeared from the scene by the time these words are read, all three Strategic Missile Wings (SMWs) which operated this weapon system having been deactivated. In contrast, Minuteman continues to be a major element of the deterrent, close to 1,000 examples of this missile remaining in use with six SMWs, although some have been removed from their silos in order to make way for the Peacekeeper ICBM. Now in the initial stages of deployment with the 90th SMW at F. E. Warren AFB, Wyoming, all 100 rounds of the new missile are to be allocated to this base following the rejection by Congress of the so-called 'dense pack' concept. The emplacement of Peacekeeper is expected to be completed in late 1989.

Looking ahead a few years, SAC has every justification for facing the future with confidence, for the Command expects to receive more new equipment during the next decade, permitting the long-overdue retirement of some of its older weapons systems. Northrop's Advanced Technology Bomber is likely to head this phase of modernization and should permit most, if not all, of the ageing B-52s to be retired at long last, while the Small ICBM will, should it come to fruition, significantly bolster SAC's missile capabilities.

92nd BW	Fairchild, Wa	325 BS	B-52H
		43/92 ARS	KC-135A
93rd BW	Castle, Ca	328 BS	B-52G
		4017 CCTS	B-52G
		93/924 ARS	KC-135A/R
96th BW	Dyess, Tx	337 BS	B-1B
		4018 CCTS	B-1B
		917 ARS	KC-135A
97th BW	Blytheville, Ar	340 BS	B-52G
		97 ARS	KC-135A
305th ARW	Grissom, In	70 ARS	KC-135A/D, EC-135G/L
		305 ARS	KC-135A/D
306th SW	RAF Mildenhall	–	TDY KC-135A/Q, RC-135U/V/W
319th BW	Grand Forks, ND	46 BS	B-1B summer 1987
		905 ARS	KC-135A
320th BW	Mather, Ca	441 BS	B-52G
321st SMW	Grand Forks, ND	446/447/448 SMS	LGM-30G
340th ARW	Altus, Ok	11/306 ARS	KC-135A
341st SMW	Malmstrom, Mt	10/12/490 SMS	LGM-30F
		564 SMS	LGM-30G
351st SMW	Whiteman, Mo	508/509/510 SMS	LGM-30F
376th SW	Kadena, Okinawa	909 ARS	KC-135A/Q/R (TDY KC-135A, RC-135)
379th BW	Wurtsmith, Mi	524 BS	B-52G
		920 ARS	KC-135A
380th BW	Plattsburgh, NY	528/529 BS	FB-111A
		4007 CCTS	FB-111A
		310/380 ARS	KC-135A/Q
384th ARW	McConnell, Ks	91†/384 ARS	KC-135R
410th BW	K. I. Sawyer, Mi	644 BS	B-52H (possibly two sqns.)
		46 ARS	KC-135A
416th BW	Griffiss, NY	668 BS	B-52G
		41 ARS	KC-135A
509th BW	Pease, NH	393/715 BS	FB-111A
		509 ARS	KC-135A

*Det. 1 Kadena SR-71A; Det. 2 Osan U-2R; Det. 3 Akrotiri U-2R; Det. 4 Mildenhall SR-71A; Det. 5 Patrick U-2R; Det. 6 Norton SR-71A? †To deactivate 1/10/87.

INDEX

Page numbers in bold type refer to illustrations